MW00999129

Hiking Guide To

THE

MISSOURI

TRAILS

Your Comprehensive Guide to
Hiking The Missouri Trails

Nelson Newman

COPYRIGHT NOTICE

DISCLAIMER

Please note that the information contained within this document is for educational purposes only. The information contained herein has been obtained from sources believed to be reliable at the time of publication. The opinions expressed herein are subject to change without notice.

Readers acknowledge that the Author / Publisher is not engaging in rendering legal, financial or professional advice. The Publisher / Author disclaims all warranties as to the accuracy, completeness, or adequacy of such information.

The Publisher assumes no liability for errors, omissions, or inadequacies in the information contained herein or from the interpretations thereof. The publisher / Author specifically disclaims any liability from the use or application of the information contained herein or from the interpretations thereof.

TABLE OF CONTENTS

INTRODUCTION

WELCOME TO THE MISSOURI HIKING TRAILS

Hey, fellow hiker! If you're reading this, you're probably just as thrilled as I am to hit the trails in Missouri. Whether you're a seasoned trekker or just getting started, you're in for an experience. Missouri, with its different landscapes and visual splendor, has something for everyone. From the rough Ozarks to the tranquil Riverways, this state is a hiker's dream.

I've spent countless hours exploring Missouri's trails, and I'm excited to share my experiences and expertise with you. This book is intended to provide a thorough guide to hiking in Missouri. We'll go over everything from picking the correct gear to exploring the state's top trails. So, lace up your boots and let's explore what makes Missouri such a great hiking destination!

Overview of the Missouri Hiking Landscape

Missouri's hiking landscape is full with natural treasures, with a variety of terrains and habitats to suit hikers of all skill levels. Imagine yourself hiking through old hardwood woods, strolling along crystal-clear rivers, or tackling difficult mountain paths. Missouri is home to the Ozark Highlands, which have rough terrain, deep valleys, and breathtaking views. This area is notable for its limestone bluffs, clean streams, and large cave systems.

The Mississippi and Missouri rivers form lovely river basins in the state's eastern region, teeming with flora and fauna. Here, you'll find routes that provide both scenic beauty and insight into the state's fascinating history. The Katy Trail, one of the country's longest rail tracks, passes through this area, giving an easy stroll through scenic terrain.

Missouri also has various state parks and conservation areas, each with its own beauty. For example, the Mark Twain National Forest, which spans 1.5 million acres, has innumerable paths that wind across various habitats. Whether you're hiking the difficult Bell Mountain Trail or the more leisurely routes in Castlewood State Park, there's always something new to explore.

Benefits of Hiking

Hiking is more than simply the physical act of walking through nature; it is a multifaceted exercise that provides several advantages. On a physical level, hiking is an excellent workout. It strengthens your muscles, promotes cardiovascular health, and increases flexibility. Hiking engages a variety of muscle groups, which helps tone your body and increase endurance.

However, the benefits of hiking extend beyond physical wellness. Hiking is an excellent technique to relieve tension and clear your thoughts. Walking's regular pace, along with the natural beauty of your surroundings, provides a contemplative experience that may considerably relieve tension and anxiety. Breathing in fresh air and listening to nature's noises might help you stay grounded and enhance your overall well-being.

Hiking also provides a mental challenge. Navigating routes, reading maps, and conquering varied terrains all stimulate your intellect in ways that regular hobbies may not. This cognitive engagement can enhance problem-solving abilities and mental sharpness. Furthermore, being outside in nature has been demonstrated to boost creativity and cognitive function, which may be quite beneficial.

Hiking may be a great social activity. Sharing these experiences, whether hiking with friends or joining a local hiking organization, fosters long-term relationships. The shared sense of success that comes from finishing a route or overcoming a problem together may improve relationships and create unforgettable memories.

How to Use This Book

This book is intended to be your ultimate companion for exploring Missouri's trails, and I want to ensure you get the most out of it. Here's a brief tutorial for navigating it:

1. Essential Gear & Equipment: We'll start with the basics of what you'll need before hitting the trails. This section covers everything from selecting appropriate footwear to packing your rucksack properly. Pay close attention to this chapter since having the proper equipment may make or ruin your hiking trip.

2. Plan Your Hike: Before you lace up your boots, you should plan your hike. This chapter will explain how to select a path, plan your itinerary, and prepare for various weather situations. Good planning ensures that your hike is both safe and pleasant.

3. Prioritize safety and preparedness when hiking. This chapter discusses important safety guidelines, how to cope with crises, and how to be prepared for many circumstances that may arise on the route.

4. Hiking Techniques & Tips: Want to trek like a pro? This section offers practical advice on hiking skills, such as how to navigate diverse terrains and manage your energy.

5. Tips for Responsible Hiking: To preserve nature and have a great experience, follow these guidelines. This chapter discusses the best hiking methods and frequent pitfalls to avoid.

6. Sample Itinerary: Not sure where to begin? Whether you are a novice, intermediate, or experienced hiker, these example itineraries will lead you to some of Missouri's greatest trails.

7. The book's main focus is on the top hiking trails in Missouri. Here, we look at Missouri's best hiking routes, from the well-known Ozark Trail to hidden treasures in nearby parks. Each trail is comprehensive, including what to expect, difficulty levels, and important points.

8. Trailer Reviews and Highlights: Dive deeper into certain trails with extensive assessments. This chapter will explain what makes each path distinctive and why it is worth investigating.

9. Discover Missouri's Natural Beauty: The state's various landscapes provide opportunities beyond hiking. This chapter delves into the vegetation, animals, and picturesque locations you may visit along the journey.

10. Seasonal Hiking Considerations: The hiking experience varies depending on the season. This chapter offers advice for trekking year-round, from spring blossoms to winter experiences.

11. Planning to hike with your pet? This section explains all you need to know about hiking with pets, including pet-friendly paths and safety precautions.

12. Family Hiking Adventures: Hiking is a great family activity. Here, we'll look at kid-friendly paths and offer advice on hiking with youngsters.

13. solitary Hiking Tips: This chapter provides tips for solitary hikers to keep safe, enjoy solitude, and maximize their experience.

14. Tips for Group Hiking: Hiking with others has unique difficulties and benefits. This chapter explains how to plan group hikes and make sure everyone has a good time.

15. Night trekking: Interested in a unique adventure? Consider night trekking. This section discusses the elements of trekking after dark, such as safety precautions and gear.

16. The COVID-19 epidemic has altered hiking practices. This chapter explains how to keep safe and follow health rules when enjoying the outdoors.

17. Advanced Hiking skills: This section covers advanced hiking skills, such as climbing and negotiating challenging terrain.

18. Maintaining Your Gear: Keeping your gear in good shape is essential. This chapter explains how to clean, maintain, and store your hiking equipment.

19. Integrating Hiking into a Fitness Routine: Learn about the health and wellbeing advantages of hiking.

20. Resources and Additional Information: This section provides a list of local hiking groups, internet networks, and forthcoming events to keep connected to the hiking community.

21. Appendix • A. Emergency Contacts: A list of key contacts in case of emergency.

• Maps and navigational tools for Missouri trails.

• C. Recommended books and articles for additional reading.

• D. Definitions of Common Hiking Terms.

• E. Apps and Tools for Hikers: Enhance your hiking experience.

Following this guide will help you prepare to conquer Missouri's trails and make the most of your hiking excursions. Each chapter is designed to give you with useful tips, insights, and inspiration to help you appreciate the great outdoors.

CHAPTER 1

ESSENTIAL GEAR AND EQUIPMENT

Hiking is as much about planning as it is about the activity itself. Having the appropriate gear may turn a difficult trip into a pleasurable one. Over the years, I've found that choosing the right footwear, clothing, bags, and other necessities makes a huge impact. Allow me to guide you through the gear and equipment that will ensure a safe and pleasurable hike.

Selecting the Right Footwear

Let's start with what's right on the ground: your shoes. A decent pair of hiking boots or shoes is essential because they give the support and traction required on varying terrain. Here's what you should look for:

• **Fit and comfort:** A proper fit is vital. When trying on hiking boots, check sure there is enough freedom to wriggle your toes without allowing your foot to slip about. You will be on your feet for long periods of time, so comfort is essential. Look for footwear that offer appropriate arch support and cushioning.

• **Type of boots:** There are several forms of hiking footwear, such as trail runners, hiking shoes, and boots. Trail runners are ideal for well-maintained routes and short walks. Hiking shoes are suitable for a variety of terrains. For difficult, uneven paths or multi-day excursions, choose robust hiking boots with ankle support.

• **Check the boots' outsole for traction.** Deep lugs offer a stronger grip on slippery or uneven surfaces. Vibram soles are renowned for their durability and traction.

• **Waterproofing:** Depending on where you'll be trekking, waterproof footwear may be required. Gore-Tex is a popular waterproof textile; nevertheless, waterproofing can impair breathability, so assess the benefits and drawbacks according on your hiking circumstances.

I remember a trek in the Ozarks where the route became a muddy mess. My boots, with superb traction and waterproofing, stopped me from slipping and getting wet feet.

Clothing for Various Weather Conditions

The appropriate apparel may significantly improve your trail comfort and performance. Layers are your greatest friend since they allow you to adapt your outfit to the weather and your level of activity.

• **The base layer,** nearest to the skin, should be moisture-wicking to prevent sweating. Merino wool and synthetic textiles such as polyester are excellent possibilities. Avoid cotton since it absorbs moisture and might make you chilly.

• **Cooler temperatures require an insulating layer.** Fleece and down are popular choices. Fleece is breathable and suitable for most circumstances, whereas down provides good warmth but loses its insulation capabilities when wet.

• **The outer layer provides protection against wind,** rain, and snow. A decent rain jacket or shell should be waterproof and breathable. Look for adjustable hoods, ventilation zippers, and a tightly cinched hem to keep drafts out.

• **Remember to bring gloves and a cap.** A wide-brimmed hat offers shade and keeps the sun off your face, while gloves protect your hands from the chill. Consider wearing a UV-protective clothing and sunglasses when going on a sunny trek.

I recall a trek through the Mark Twain National Forest where the weather changed significantly. I was able to keep warm despite the unexpected downpour and chilly gusts because to my variable layering technique.

Backpacks: Their Features

Your backpack is effectively a movable base camp. It should be comfortable, sturdy, and appropriate for the length of your walk. Here's what you should look for:

• Day treks typically demand a pack with a capacity of 20-30 liters. Overnight or multi-day treks require a heavier pack, often 40-70 liters. Make sure the pack is large enough to hold your goods but not so bulky that you wind up carrying too much weight.

• Comfortable backpacks include adjustable shoulder straps, cushioned hip belt, and sternum strap. These elements assist to distribute weight evenly and reduce pain. Adjust the straps so the pack fits firmly on your back and does not swing.

• **Choose a bag with numerous sections for simple management.** Side pockets, hydration sleeves, and a top lid pocket are all quite handy features. Some bags additionally have front or side zippers for easy access to commonly used goods.

• Backpacks often have a hydration reservoir sleeve and hose for convenient drinking on the go. Alternatively, you can utilize water bottles that fit in the side pockets.

On a recent trek along the Katy Trail, my pack's hydration reservoir and side pockets made it easy to get snacks and drink, enabling me to appreciate the landscape.

Navigation Tools: Maps, Compasses, and GPS

Getting lost is not on anybody's bucket list. Proper navigation tools will keep you on the correct track:

• Always have a thorough map of the trekking region. Topographic maps are particularly valuable since they depict elevation variations and geographical characteristics. Learn to read maps and identify contour lines and symbols.

• **A compass is a useful tool for orienting and navigating** when lost. Before you go hiking, practice using it. Remember, a compass is only effective if you understand how to use it in combination with a map.

• **Smartphone applications and handheld GPS gadgets** can be quite useful. They provide real-time location monitoring and can guide you through complicated paths. However, do not rely entirely on electronic gadgets. Always have a backup plan in case batteries expire or signals fail.

On less-traveled paths, the GPS has saved my life several times. Still, I always carry a map and compass as a backup in case technology fails.

Hydration and Food Supply

Staying hydrated and well-fed is essential for sustaining energy levels on the course.

• **Pack enough water for your hike.** For shorter treks, a water bottle or two will serve. Longer hikes benefit from a hydration reservoir or large capacity water bottles. If you'll be using natural water sources, consider carrying a water filter or purification tablets.

• **Pack healthful,** lightweight meals to offer energy. Trail mix, energy bars, and dried fruit are excellent choices. For longer walks, pack compact, calorie-dense meals that are simple to cook. If you wish to cook, remember to bring a tiny, portable stove.

• **Cooking Gear:** Bring a lightweight stove, fuel, and utensils. Choose a small burner that fits easily into your bag and has a pot suitable for the meals you intend to make.

A well-planned food supply and dependable hydration system made a big difference on a lengthy hiking trip in the Ozarks. It helped me keep motivated and focused on the course.

First-aid kits and emergency equipment

Accidents happen, and being prepared might mean the difference. Here's what you should include in your first aid kit and emergency equipment:

• **Basic goods for a first aid kit include adhesive bandages,** antiseptic wipes, gauze pads, medical tape, tweezers, scissors, and pain medicines. Customize your gear based on the duration of your journey and the number of persons in your group.

• **Emergency gear includes a whistle,** multi-tool, fire starter, and flashlight/headlamp. A fire starter can save your life if you need to create a fire during a survival crisis. A whistle may be used to summon assistance if necessary, and a torch or headlamp allows you to see and be seen in low light conditions.

• **Survival items:** Consider bringing a tiny emergency shelter or space blanket. These goods can protect you from the elements if you find yourself in an unexpected circumstance.

On one trek, I came across a fellow hiker who had injured his ankle. My first-aid package enabled me to offer prompt assistance and get them back to the trailhead. Being prepared with these items might make a significant difference in such situations.

Final Thoughts

Having the appropriate clothing and equipment is essential for a safe and pleasurable hiking trip. A well-prepared hiker must have proper footwear, clothes, backpacks, navigation gadgets, hydration and food supplies, and first-aid kit. You'll be set up for numerous great treks and experiences if you take the time to pick and understand your gear.

So, get your gear ready, and let's go explore Missouri's gorgeous trails. The adventures that await you are definitely worth the preparation!

CHAPTER 2

PLAN YOUR HIKE

Planning a trek is more than simply choosing a path and turning there. It's about putting yourself in the best possible position to enjoy your experience. A well-thought-out itinerary might be the difference between a relaxing, pleasurable trek and an unexpected hardship. Let's go over the fundamental elements for preparing your trek, from setting goals to packing your kit.

Setting Goals for Your Hike

Before you lace up your boots and hit the path, be sure you have clear goals for your trip. This will help you plan and ensure a satisfying encounter. Here's how to create successful goals:

• **Determine your fitness level.** Evaluate your fitness level objectively. Are you an experienced hiker searching for a challenge, or a novice looking for a more leisurely outing? Your fitness level will influence the path difficulty and length that's best for you.

Determine the type of hike: Are you planning on a day trek, a weekend backpacking trip, or a multi-day expedition? Your aim will determine the length of the path, the type of equipment required, and the amount of food and water you'll bring.

• **Consider your interests.** Consider what interests you the most. Are you drawn to beautiful scenery, animals, or historic sites? Tailoring your trek to your preferences will make it more pleasurable.

• **Set attainable milestones:** If you're preparing for a certain event or want to enhance your hiking abilities, make short, attainable goals. This may entail hiking a set number of kilometers every week or conquering more difficult paths.

When I initially started hiking, my main aim was to enjoy the outdoors and improve my fitness. As I acquired expertise, I began to set more precise goals, such as finishing a difficult multi-day walk in the Ozarks. These goals kept me motivated and allowed me to measure my progress.

Researching Trails and Destinations

Once you've decided on your goals, you may start researching paths and locations. This phase is critical for ensuring that you pick a trek that corresponds with your goals and tastes.

• **Use trail guides and maps.** Look for trail guides, maps, and internet resources that have thorough information on different paths. Pay attention to path length, elevation gain, difficulty level, and distinguishing features.

• **Read trail reviews.** Check out the reviews of other hikers. They can give vital information on trail conditions, recent changes, and what to expect. Websites like AllTrails and local hiking forums are excellent sources for this.

• **Consider accessibility.** Consider how far you're willing to drive to reach the trailhead. Some trails may be a short drive away, while others may need a longer journey. Make sure you consider the time and effort necessary to get there.

• **Explore trail features.** Find out about the trail's characteristics. Are there any picturesque viewpoints, waterfalls, or historical landmarks? Knowing what to expect might help you decide whether the path is suitable for your interests and goals.

I recall looking for paths for a hiking trip in the Mark Twain National Forest. Reading reviews and looking at maps helped me find a path with beautiful views and a moderate difficulty level that suited my fitness objectives and interest in gorgeous surroundings.

Developing a Hiking Plan

After you've decided on a path, you'll need to plan out your hike in detail. This strategy will lead you through the trek while keeping you safe:

• **Plan your route:** Mark the beginning and finish places of your hike on a map. Make a note of any crossroads or other routes you may encounter. If you're going on a multi-day trek, organize your stops and campsites.

• **Estimated time:** Calculate how long it will take to complete the trek based on your speed and path difficulties. Allow additional time for breaks, meals, and unforeseen delays. As a general rule, allow more time than you anticipate.

• **Check trail conditions.** Check the current trail conditions and any closures or restrictions. Local park websites and visitor centers can give up-to-date information on trail conditions, weather, and other relevant factors.

• **Share your plan:** Always notify someone of your trek plans, including your start and end timings and estimated return. This is critical for safety in the event something goes wrong.

On a recent trip along the Ozark Trail, I carefully planned my route and approximated the time necessary. Sharing my itinerary with a companion and researching trail conditions ahead facilitated a smooth and safe experience.

Permissions and Regulations

Some trails and parks need permits or have special rules that you must observe. To avoid problems, it is critical to be aware of the following requirements:

• **Check permit requirements.** Some popular or protected sites require permits to hike or camp. Check with your local land management agency or park service to determine whether you need to get a permit in advance.

• **Understand regulations.** Familiarize yourself with any park or trail laws. This might include restrictions governing campfires, rubbish disposal, or pet policies. Following these standards contributes to the preservation of the natural environment while also providing a pleasant experience for everybody.

• **Reserve Campsites:** If your trek includes camping, plan ahead of time. Many famous routes have designated camping spots, which fill up rapidly, particularly during high season.

I learnt the value of permits and rules the hard way when I arrived at a trailhead only to discover that permits were necessary. Fortunately, I was able to obtain a permit online, but the experience taught me the value of planning ahead of time.

Weather Considerations

Weather may make or break a trek, therefore it's critical to check the weather and plan accordingly:

• **Check the forecast.** Check the weather prediction in the days preceding up to your hike and on the day of the walk. Look for temperature ranges, precipitation probabilities, and wind conditions.

• **Prepare for changes.** Weather may be unpredictable, particularly in hilly or wooded places. Bring clothing layers to adjust to shifting circumstances and be ready for unforeseen weather changes.

• **Understand the risks:** Be mindful of weather-related hazards such as lightning, severe temperatures, and flash floods. If bad weather is forecast, you may want to postpone your trek or choose a another route.

During a spring trek in the Mark Twain National Forest, I experienced a surprise rainfall. Fortunately, I had brought a rain jacket and extra layers to keep me dry and comfortable.

Packing Checklist

Now that you've planned your hike, it's time to prepare your supplies. Here's a detailed checklist to make sure you have everything you need:

• **Backpack:** Choose a pack that is comfortable and has adequate space for your things. Make sure it's well-organized and that commonly used goods are easily accessible.

• **Pack moisture-wicking base layers,** an insulating layer, and a waterproof upper layer. Include a hat, gloves, and additional socks.

• **Pack appropriate hiking boots or shoes for the terrain.** Consider bringing an extra pair of socks to keep your feet dry.

• **Navigation tools include a map,** compass, and GPS gadget. If you're using electronic navigation equipment, make sure they're completely charged and have backup batteries on hand if needed.

• **Bring adequate water for the trek.** If you're using a hydration reservoir, make sure it's full and the hose works correctly. If you use water bottles, be sure they are tight and leak-proof.

• **Bring energy-dense foods such as trail mix,** energy bars, and dried fruits. For longer walks, bring meals that are simple to cook and transport.

• Prepare a basic first aid kit with bandages, antiseptic wipes, gauze, and pain medications. Customize your gear to meet your needs and the length of your walk.

• **Pack emergency gear,** including a whistle, multi-tool, fire starter, and flashlight or headlamp. Ensure that these goods are immediately available in the event of an emergency.

• **Bring sunscreen,** bug repellent, a camera, and a journal for recording observations and comments.

I recall one trek where a fellow hiker failed to carry enough water. They had to shorten their hike, which might have been prevented with a detailed packing list. Having all of the necessary supplies not only makes the trek more fun, but it also guarantees that you are prepared for any eventuality.

Final Thoughts

Effective planning is essential for a successful climb. Setting clear goals, studying routes, developing a precise strategy, comprehending permits and rules, taking into account the weather, and packing properly prepares you for a fun and safe hiking excursion. Every stage of the preparation process helps to make the journey go more smoothly, letting you to enjoy the trail's beauty and thrill.

So, take your time planning, and you'll be rewarded with wonderful treks and experiences. Now that you have the information to prepare properly, it's time to bring it all together and hit the trails with confidence!

CHAPTER 3

SAFETY AND

PREPARATION

When I lace up my hiking boots, I always have safety and readiness in mind. Whether you're on a well-traveled road or an unexplored one, understanding how to be safe and manage crises is essential. Let's look at the most important parts of hiking safety, including route signs and basic first aid.

Understanding Trail Markings and Signs

Trail markers and signage lead you through the woods, helping you remain on course and make educated decisions.

• **Trail markers include blazes,** paint, and signs. Blazes are usually colorful marks on trees or rocks. In the United States, a single colored blaze typically signifies the main path, although numerous blazes or various colors may indicate intersections or branch trails. Learn the marking system for the path you're hiking.

• **path signs give crucial information** such as path names, lengths, and directions. Pay attention to the signage at trailheads, crossroads, and key turns. They frequently identify the difficulty of the terrain, the projected trek duration, and safety cautions.

• **Guideposts with maps and information** are available at crucial spots along several routes. Keep an eye out for these and use them to validate your location and navigate through junctions.

On a trek through the Ozark Highlands, I came upon a route with a combination of blazes and markers. Knowing how to interpret these marks allowed me to travel the path more effectively and avoid getting lost.

Wildlife Safety

Encounters with wildlife may be fascinating, but they can carry hazards. Here's how to be safe among animals:

• **Research the fauna you may see on your journey.** In Missouri, you may see deer, black bears, or even dangerous snakes. Understanding their behavior and routines allows you to react accordingly.

• **Avoid feeding wildlife.** Feeding animals can cause violent behavior and disturb their normal foraging patterns. Always keep your food safe and don't try to lure wildlife with snacks.

• **When trekking in bear-prone areas,** use bear-proof food containers and maintain a clean campsite to ensure safety. Make noise when trekking to avoid startling a bear.

• **Be cautious near rocks and underbrush,** as snakes may be lurking. If you encounter a snake, be cool and allow it to go away.

During a trek in the Ozark National Scenic Riverways, I saw a black bear from a distance. Following safety rules (making noise and keeping my distance) resulted in a safe and courteous interaction.

Dealing With Weather Challenges

Weather might change quickly, affecting your hike greatly. Being prepared for diverse circumstances is key.

· **Check the weather forecast before venturing** out to be prepared for unexpected events. Prepare for unexpected changes by carrying rain gear, additional clothes, and sun protection. Temperatures in mountainous places may drop fast, so wearing the appropriate gear can help prevent hypothermia.

• **Heat and hydration:** Stay hydrated during hot weather and take rests in the shade. Heat exhaustion and dehydration may happen fast, particularly on severe walks. Drink plenty of fluids and keep an eye out for any indications of heat sickness.

• **In chilly conditions,** layer clothing and prevent exposed skin from frostbite. A windproof and waterproof outer layer is essential for keeping you warm and dry.

• **When a thunderstorm approaches,** take quick cover. Avoid towering trees, broad fields, and metallic items. If you're trapped in the open, squat down with your feet together and avoid contacting the ground with your arms.

I remember a trek where the weather became bad, with heavy rain and high gusts. Packing a weather-resistant jacket and extra layers kept me dry and comfortable until the weather changed.

What to do in case of an emergency

Emergencies can occur, and understanding how to respond can make a significant difference.

• **Remain calm:** Panic can worsen a problem. Be cool and examine the situation before acting. Clear thinking enables you to make better selections.

• **Assess the situation.** Determine the nature of the emergency. Is it a medical concern, a missing hiker, or a weather-related issue? Understanding the situation allows you to determine the best line of action.

• **Use a whistle or mirror to signal for help.** In places with cell coverage, contact emergency services. Please include your location and information about the incident.

• **Provide first assistance to wounded individuals.** Follow the instructions in your first aid package and keep track of the wounded person's status.

On a trek in the Ozarks, I assisted a fellow hiker who had twisted his ankle. By remaining cool, examining the damage, and utilizing my first aid pack, I was able to administer immediate care and get them to safety.

Basic First Aid Skills

Basic first aid skills are essential for managing common accidents and medical conditions on the trail:

• **Clean wounds and cuts with water and apply antiseptic.** To prevent infection, wrap the wound with sterile cloths. For serious wounds or excessive bleeding, apply pressure with a clean towel and seek medical attention right once.

• **Prevent blisters with good footwear and moisture-wicking socks.** If you develop a blister, cover it with a blister pad or bandage and prevent bursting it, which can lead to infection.

• **For mild sprains and strains,** use ice to minimize swelling and an elastic bandage for support. Rest and elevate the afflicted region, if possible. Seek medical assistance if you have severe injuries or are experiencing persistent discomfort.

• **If someone exhibits indications of dehydration** or heat exhaustion, move them to a shady or cool place, administer drinks, and monitor their status. The symptoms include dizziness, nausea, and profuse perspiration.

I once utilized these first aid abilities on a summer trip when a group member became very dehydrated. We successfully managed the issue by moving immediately and giving refreshments and shade.

Communication and Navigation Safety on the path requires effective communication and navigation skills

• **Stay in touch:** If you're hiking with a group, figure out how to communicate and keep track of where everyone is. Agree on meeting sites in the event of separation.

• **Use a GPS gadget or smartphone app** to remain on track and traverse unknown paths. Make sure your smartphone is fully charged and keep backup batteries on hand in case you need them.

• **Familiarize** yourself with the route before setting out. Examine maps and route descriptions to better grasp major spots, intersections, and markers.

• **Learn basic map reading skills.** Knowing how to read a map and use a compass is really useful. Practice these skills so you can navigate efficiently even when your technological devices fail.

I've been on numerous walks when solid communication and navigation skills were critical. On a multi-day hiking trip, having a GPS gadget and understanding how to utilize a map kept us on track and prevented unnecessary diversions.

Final Thoughts

Safety and preparation are essential components of a successful hiking trip. Understanding trail signs, practicing animal safety, planning for weather problems, knowing how to manage crises, learning basic first aid, and improving communication and navigation skills prepares you to deal with the unexpected and fully enjoy your trek.

So, take these safety guidelines to heart, prepare adequately, and head out into the path with confidence.

CHAPTER 4

HIKING TECHNIQUES AND

TIPS

When I go hiking, I don't merely put one foot in front of the other. There's a lot more to it—techniques and recommendations for making each step more effective, each climb more doable, and each encounter more delightful. I've learnt these strategies from years of hiking various routes and am eager to share them with you. Let's look at the basics of appropriate hiking posture, effective tactics, and how to navigate various terrains.

Proper Hiking Posture

Good posture is essential for a relaxing and productive trek. It influences how you navigate the terrain, preserve energy, and avoid injury.

• **Keep your back straight.** Maintaining a straight back distributes your weight evenly and relieves pressure on your spine. Avoid leaning forward or hunching over, especially on an uphill.

• **Strengthen your core to support** your lower back and maintain stability. Engage your abdominal muscles while hiking to maintain proper posture and prevent fatigue.

• **Relax your shoulders and avoid tensing them.** Tension in the shoulders can cause discomfort and stiffness over time.

• **Make sure your backpack is correctly fitted.** The weight should be evenly distributed on your back, with the straps snug but not overly tight. This helps you stay balanced and relieves stress on your shoulders and hips.

When I initially started hiking, I frequently found myself leaning forward on steep hills, resulting in back discomfort and tiredness. My climbs became much more pleasant and pleasurable as I focused on keeping a straight posture and using my core.

Effective Hiking Techniques

Efficiency on the route entails spending less energy to cover greater distance. Here are some ways to increase your efficiency:

• **Pace yourself:** Find a speed that is both comfortable and sustainable for the duration of the hike. Avoid hurrying, since it might cause early weariness. Instead, aim for a consistent beat that fits your fitness level.

• **Use a three-point stance.** On steep or rough terrain, take a three-point stance, with one hand on your knee or a trekking pole for added support. This method helps to balance your body and lessens the strain on your legs.

• **Use a zigzag pattern:** When ascending steep hills, consider trekking in a zigzag manner rather than straight up the incline. This decreases the grade, making the ascent less arduous.

- **Minimize steps on flat terrain by taking** longer strides instead of small ones. This allows you to cover more ground with less effort.

During a difficult ascent in the Ozark Mountains, I discovered that employing a zigzag pattern with trekking poles allowed me to ascend more effectively and preserve energy for the remainder of the walk.

Navigating Different Terrain

Each type of terrain provides unique obstacles. Knowing how to deal with them will make your walk safer and more enjoyable:

- **When trekking in rocky terrain,** utilize bigger rocks for stability. Look out for loose or unstable rocks that might cause slips and falls. Use trekking poles to improve your balance.

- **Muddy and slippery trails:** On wet or slippery terrain, take fewer steps and arrange your feet carefully to prevent slipping. If the track is really slick, try employing cleats or spikes to increase traction.

• **When hiking on sandy or loose dirt trails,** prioritize packed parts. Take smaller, more careful steps to avoid sinking or sliding.

• **When crossing streams or rivers,** use walking sticks or trekking poles to determine the depth and stability of the water. Cross in specified spots if available, and always prioritize safety.

I recall traversing a particularly muddy route in the Mark Twain National Forest. I easily navigated the muddy areas by taking short steps and using trekking poles for support.

Managing Fatigue and Energy

Managing your energy and dealing with exhaustion are essential for a good trek. Here's how to stay energetic and prevent burnout:

• **Stay hydrated:** Drink water on a regular basis, even if you are not thirsty. Dehydration can cause weariness and poor performance. Drink in modest amounts regularly rather than in huge quantities all at once.

• **Pack energy-boosting foods like almonds,** energy bars, and dried fruit. These foods help you maintain your energy levels and avoid mid-hike tiredness.

• **Take breaks:** Make regular stops to relax, hydrate, and refuel. Short, frequent breaks are frequently more beneficial than longer, less frequent ones. Take these moments to stretch and reduce muscular tension.

• **Listen to your body:** Pay attention to how you're feeling and alter your speed or take extra breaks as necessary. Pushing through weariness might result in injury or a more challenging hike.

On a particularly tough climb, I learnt the value of taking regular pauses and staying hydrated. By stopping to relax and eat, I was able to finish the trek feeling considerably better than if I had tried to press through without interruptions.

Using Trekking Poles

Trekking poles may be really useful on the route. They provide stability, decrease impact, and make your trip more comfortable:

- **Adjust pole length.** Set your trekking poles to the suitable length for the terrain. The poles should be shorter for uphill climbs and longer for downhill descents to maintain balance.

- **Use Proper Technique:** Place trekking poles firmly in front of you when walking. To ascend, use the poles to press against the terrain. They are useful for absorbing shock and maintaining equilibrium during descent.

- **Use alternating poles with opposing foot** to replicate natural walking rhythm. This method improves balance and decreases strain on your legs.

- To minimize stumbling and preserve energy, fold or store poles when not in use, especially over flat terrain.

I've discovered that utilizing trekking poles on steep descents not only improves my balance, but also decreases pressure on my knees. The poles were very useful on a difficult terrain, providing stability and support.

Leave No Trace Principles

Every hiker bears some responsibility for environmental preservation. Follow the Leave No Trace guidelines to maintain the trails lovely for future hikers.

• **Pack out all trash.** Take out all rubbish, including food leftovers and packaging. If you see litter left by others, clean it up if feasible. This helps to maintain the route clean and enjoyable for everybody.

• **Respect wildlife by observing them** from a distance and not disrupting their natural activities. To avoid attracting wildlife, keep food in a secure location and properly dispose of rubbish.

• **Stay on designated trails.** To minimize environmental effect, stick to existing routes. Avoid developing new routes or shortcuts since they might lead to erosion and habitat loss.

• **Camp Responsibly:** Use designated campsites and observe restrictions for fires and rubbish disposal. Leave the campground cleaner than you found it.

I make it a point to observe Leave No Trace principles on every trek. This not only helps to safeguard the ecosystem, but also assures that future hikers may enjoy the same breathtaking scenery that I do.

Final Thoughts

Mastering hiking skills and advice requires work, but it makes a huge difference in your trekking experience. From keeping appropriate posture and traversing diverse terrains to controlling energy levels and properly utilizing trekking poles, these skills improve both your safety and pleasure on the trail.

So, take these strategies to heart, use them on your treks, and see how they change your outdoor activities. With the appropriate attitude, every trek can be an amazing and rewarding experience, and you'll be more equipped to face anything the route throws at you. Happy trekking!

CHAPTER 5

DO'S AND DON'TS FOR HIKING

Hiking is more than just putting one foot in front of another. I've learnt over the years that following a set of best practices and avoiding frequent errors may significantly improve the experience. Whether you're a seasoned hiker or a beginner, knowing these dos and don'ts may make your outdoor activities safer, more pleasant, and respectful of the natural environment and other hikers. Let's get into the basic rules for a good hiking trip.

Safe Hiking Practices

Responsible hiking habits are the cornerstone of a satisfying hiking experience. Here's how to be a responsible hiker.

• **Plan ahead:** Before starting out, do some research on your selected path. Understand the trail's difficulty, duration, and any particular requirements, such as seasonal restrictions or wildlife activity. A well-planned trek guarantees that you are prepared and capable of dealing with any obstacles that may arise.

• **Know and follow regulations:** Each trail and park may have its own set of rules. These might include campfire limits, dedicated camping sites, or pet-specific laws. Familiarize yourself with these rules and obey them to conserve the environment and have a safe trek.

• **Respect trail closures.** Trails might be closed for repair, animal protection, or other reasons. Respect the closures to prevent causing trail damage or disturbing wildlife. If the path or trail you intended to hike is closed, always find an alternative.

• **Stay on marked trails.** Following defined paths helps to reduce habitat loss and erosion. Creating additional pathways or cutting corners might harm sensitive ecosystems and cause soil erosion. Stick to the approved route to maintain the area's natural beauty.

I recall a trek where I selected a trail that was temporarily closed for renovation. It was tempting to push through, but following the closure not only protected the path, but also helped to avoid potential perils.

Common Mistakes to Avoid

Avoiding common hiking blunders may significantly improve your hiking experience. Here are some hazards to look out for:

• **Overestimate your abilities:** It is easy to overestimate your fitness level or hiking expertise, especially when confronted with a difficult terrain. Choose paths appropriate for your skill level and physical condition. If you're new to hiking, start with easy routes and work your way up.

• **Ignoring weather conditions:** It's important to plan for unpredictable weather. Check the weather forecast before your trek and be ready for unexpected changes. Ignoring weather conditions might result in perilous scenarios or ruin your excursion.

• **Overpacking or under packing:** Too much weight will slow you down and cause tiredness, while under packing might leave you without crucial equipment or supplies. Strike a balance between packing essentials and eliminating superfluous stuff. Always bring adequate water, food, and suitable attire.

• **Neglecting trail safety procedures,** such as checking markers and having a map, might result in becoming lost or in dangerous situations. Prioritize safety by remaining aware of your surroundings and having navigation equipment.

On one trek, I underestimated my capacity to manage a difficult path, resulting in weariness midway through. Learning to honestly assess my skills and plan appropriately has made my hikes more fun and achievable.

Trail Etiquette

Good trail etiquette ensures that everyone has a great experience on the path. Here's how to be a respectful hiker:

• **Give to Others:** Apply the idea of "uphill hiker has the right of way." If you're descending and see hikers climbing, move aside to let them pass. This civility helps to avoid accidents and makes the journey more pleasurable for everybody.

• **Keep noise to a minimum.** Enjoying nature entails minimizing noise levels. Loud talks or music may disturb wildlife and other hikers. Maintain a calm, courteous tone and keep all electronic gadgets on mute.

• **Control Your Pets:** Keep your dog on a leash and under control when hiking. Not all hikers or wildlife welcome a friendly canine approach, and unrestrained canines can endanger themselves and others.

• **Respect personal space:** Allow other hikers to enjoy their journey without feeling crowded. Avoid getting too near to people or disrupting their experience.

During a popular weekend trek, I came across a group playing loud music. While it was evident they were having a good time, their noise disturbed the serenity of others. Adhering to trail etiquette guarantees that everyone may enjoy the beauty of nature.

Ecological Considerations

Hiking requires careful environmental considerations. Here's how to reduce your impact.

• **Follow Leave No Trace principles:** The Leave No Trace principles help you limit your environmental effect. This includes removing all waste, not plucking flora or upsetting wildlife, and utilizing established campsites.

• **Use established pathways** and sturdy surfaces to prevent erosion and damage to plants. Avoid going off track or harming vulnerable areas like meadows or wetlands.

• **Dispose of waste properly.** If there are no bathrooms accessible, pack out human waste. To dispose of sanitary waste, dig a shallow hole (6-8 inches deep) and cover it after usage.

• **Use eco-friendly products,** such as biodegradable soaps and shampoos, while washing in natural water sources. Avoid utilizing goods that may affect aquatic environments.

On a trek beside a river, I came upon a group who had left behind rubbish. It served as a sharp reminder of the significance of adhering to environmental rules in order to preserve our trails and natural beauty.

Interacting with Other Hikers

Interacting with other hikers may be a highlight of the walk. Here's how to handle these conversations respectfully:

• **Be polite and cordial with fellow hikers,** greeting them with a smile or nod. Small acts of kindness may make hiking more pleasurable for everyone.

• **Use straightforward and respectful communication** when passing someone or announcing your presence. A simple "Hello, I'm coming up behind you" can avoid surprises and assure safety.

• **Deal with problems calmly and politely,** such as those related to trail usage or personal space. Concentrate on identifying a solution that works for everyone involved.

• **Share trail information.** If you've recently hiked the same path and have any useful information, such as conditions or risks, share it with others you meet. This is especially important for visitors and people unfamiliar with the region.

During a recent trek, I had a great conversation with another hiker regarding trail conditions. They enjoyed the information, which encouraged a sense of community on the route.

Final Thoughts

Understanding and following the dos and don'ts of hiking guarantees that your outdoor experiences are not only fun but also environmentally and socially responsible. By adhering to safe hiking practices, avoiding frequent errors, respecting trail etiquette, conserving the environment, and engaging courteously with others, you may help everyone have a pleasant hiking experience.

So, keep these things in mind as you tackle the trails. They'll help you manage your walks more easily, avoid frequent traps, and make each trip a memorable and enjoyable adventure. Happy hiking, and remember that the finest hikes are those that leave both the path and the hikers in better shape than they found them.

CHAPTER 6

SAMPLE ITINERARY FOR BEGINNERS

Taking on a hiking expedition for the first time may be both exciting and intimidating. I recall my first days on the trail, when each new path seemed like unexplored country. It is critical to begin with treks that fit your skill level and progressively gain confidence. In this chapter, I'll walk you through several fantastic itineraries designed especially for beginners. Whether you're searching for simple day walks, family-friendly trails, beginner-friendly multi-day treks, or picturesque routes with few obstacles, these options will help you ease into the world of hiking.

Easy Day Hikes

Easy day treks are ideal for starting started. They have moderate distances and mild terrain, so you can build endurance and enjoy the experience without feeling overwhelmed.

- **Garden of the Gods at Shawnee National Forest in Illinois**

Distance: 1.5 miles.

Duration: 1 to 2 hours

Highlights: The Garden of the Gods Trail is a short, picturesque trek that offers breathtaking rock formations and panoramic vistas. The track is well-marked and generally level, making it suitable for novices. Don't miss the famed Observation Trail, which provides stunning views of the surrounding area.

- **The Laurel Falls Trail in Great Smoky Mountains National Park,** Tennessee/North Carolina, is 2.6 miles round-trip and takes 1-1.5 hours to complete.

Highlights: This popular route goes to a stunning waterfall and is paved for the majority of the journey, making it suitable for all ability levels. The trail is simple to follow and provides a tranquil setting ideal for a leisurely day stroll.

• **Missouri's Ozark National Scenic Riverways includes Alley Spring and Mill.**

Distance: one mile.

Duration: one hour.

Highlights: This short circle leads to the lovely Alley Spring and antique mill. The walk is easy and generally level, with stops to see the bright blue waters and examine the ancient architecture.

When I first started hiking, I discovered that picking simple paths allowed me to enjoy nature without worrying too much about the physical hardship. These pathways are ideal for learning to hike and appreciating the beauty of the outdoors.

Family Friendly Trails

Hiking with your family may be a fantastic bonding experience. Family-friendly paths are intended to be safe, enjoyable, and practicable for hikers of all ages.

- **Cunningham Falls at Catoctin Mountain Park in Maryland**

Distance: 1.5 miles.

Duration: one hour.

Highlights: The route leads to Cunningham Falls, Maryland's biggest waterfall. The walkway is well-maintained and appropriate for youngsters. The waterfalls are breathtaking, and there's lots of space for picnics and exploring.

- **The Bear Lake Trail in Rocky Mountain National Park,** Colorado, is 0.6 miles round-trip and takes 30 minutes to complete.

Highlights: The Bear Lake Trail is a short, easy stroll around a beautiful lake with spectacular mountain views. The route is paved and accessible, making it ideal for families with little children or strollers.

- **Mirror Lake Trail,** Yosemite National Park, California Distance: 2 miles (round-trip) Duration: 1-2 hours Highlights: Mirror Lake reflects the renowned granite cliffs of Yosemite. The landscape is generally level, with only a few modest inclines, making it an ideal trek for families.

I recall bringing my own children on family-friendly paths and watching their joy as they discovered new areas. These trails are intended to be interesting and manageable for all family members, allowing for the creation of long-lasting memories without undue strain.

Beginner-Friendly Multi-Day Hikes

Beginner-friendly multi-day walks allow hikers to explore more territory without encountering too much difficulties.

• **Appalachian Trail, Georgia:** Springer Mountain to Stover Creek Shelter.

Distance: 8.5 miles.

Duration: 1–2 days

Highlights: This portion of the Appalachian Trail provides a mild start to multi-day hiking. It boasts stunning woodland vistas and modest elevation climbs. Stover Creek Shelter offers a nice overnight stay.

• **California's John Muir Trail runs from Yosemite Valley to Tuolumne Meadows.**

Distance: 11 miles.

Duration: two days.

Highlights: This section of the John Muir Trail provides a magnificent tour across Yosemite's various landscapes. The path has easy rises and descents, with campsites accessible along the way. It's a fantastic introduction to longer backpacking adventures.

• **Hocking Hills State Park, Ohio - Old Man's Cave Loop.**

Distance: six miles.

Duration: 1–2 days

Highlights: The Old Man's Cave Loop has amazing rock formations, waterfalls, and beautiful woodlands. While the circle may be done in a single day, it's ideal for an overnight stay at a nearby campground to enjoy a multi-day trek without being too challenging.

Starting with beginner-friendly multi-day walks was an excellent method for me to improve my endurance and gain a taste for longer treks. These trips are of reasonable length and provide an opportunity to master the fundamentals of multi-day hiking, such as packing, setting up camp, and managing your food and water supplies.

Scenic Routes with Minimal Challenge

Scenic trails with little difficulty are ideal for novices who wish to enjoy the beauty of hiking without being unduly demanding.

• Blue Ridge Parkway, North Carolina/Virginia - Linville Falls Trail (1.6 miles)

Duration: one hour.

Highlights: This simple route leads to multiple views of the breathtaking Linville Falls. The trail is generally flat with a few modest climbs, providing stunning views of the waterfalls and surrounding environment.

• Zion National Park, Utah - Riverside Walk

Distance: 2.2 miles (round-trip) Time: 1-1.5 hours

Highlights: The Riverside Walk track, which follows the Virgin River to the Narrows entrance, is quite straightforward. It provides stunning views of the river and nearby rocks without any substantial height changes.

• Maui, Hawaii - Iao Valley State Park (0.6 miles, 30 minutes)

Highlights: This short trek at Iao Valley State Park offers breathtaking views of the famed Iao Needle and the green valley. The route is paved and simple to follow, making it excellent for anyone seeking a picturesque stroll.

Choosing beautiful paths with modest difficulty allowed me to appreciate the natural beauty of many settings without the physical effort of more difficult walks. These trails are ideal for taking in the environment and having a peaceful hiking experience.

Final Thoughts

Starting your hiking adventure with the appropriate itinerary will significantly improve how much you enjoy your time on the trails. Easy day walks, family-friendly paths, beginner-friendly multi-day treks, and scenic routes with few obstacles provide a variety of alternatives to suit varied interests and ability levels.

You will acquire confidence and create unforgettable outdoor experiences by selecting walks that are appropriate for your level of experience and gradually developing your abilities. So, lace up your boots, pack your kit, and prepare to explore the trails. Your hiking expedition awaits, and with these sample itineraries, you'll be well-prepared for a memorable and rewarding experience. Happy trekking!

CHAPTER 7

SAMPLE ITINERARY FOR INTERMEDIATE HIKERS

As you gain skill on the trails, you'll be ready to tackle increasingly difficult and rewarding hikes. Intermediate hikers frequently seek out routes that provide greater excitement, whether through moderate day hikes, weekend vacations, or multi-day excursions. In this chapter, I'll discuss a variety of routes geared for intermediate hikers who want to test their limitations while still enjoying the adventure. These routes, which range from modest day walks to tough multi-day treks, will allow you to refine your abilities while also immersing yourself in the majesty of nature.

Moderate Day Hikes

Moderate day walks find a balance of difficulty and fun. They generally entail longer distances, more elevation gain, or different terrain, but they may still be completed in a single day.

The Dipsea Trail leads from Mount Tamalpais State Park in California to Stinson Beach.

Distance: 6.5 miles.

Duration: 4–5 hours

Highlights: The Dipsea Trail provides breathtaking views of the Pacific Ocean, undulating hills, and lush woods. The path descends from Mount Tamalpais to Stinson Beach and offers a diversity of terrain. It's a moderately difficult hike with some steep portions and rough terrain, making it suitable for individuals who want to challenge their stamina without committing to a multi-day trip.

• **Rocky Mountain National Park, Colorado: Alberta Falls and Mills Lake.**

Distance: 5.5 miles (round-trip) Time: 3-4 hours

Highlights: This hike incorporates the splendor of Alberta Falls and the picturesque Mills Lake. The trail climbs steadily, passing through pine woods and alpine meadows. The views of the lake and nearby peaks are definitely worth the effort. It's an excellent alternative for people seeking a little extra challenge without a very difficult ascent.

• **Old Rag Mountain near Shenandoah National Park in Virginia.**

Distance: nine miles.

Duration: 5–7 hours

Highlights: Old Rag Mountain is famous for its rugged scrambles and breathtaking views. The climb involves a difficult rock scramble near the peak, which adds an exciting aspect to the adventure. The prize is a stunning view from the summit, making it a worthwhile trek for intermediate hikers looking for a little extra thrill.

I've always thought that moderate day treks provide an ideal balance of difficulty and pleasure. They allow you to test your limitations while yet returning home the same day, feeling successful and delighted.

Weekend getaways

Weekend trips are ideal for intermediate hikers looking to spend more time in nature. These itineraries often include longer hikes with the option of camping or staying at local lodgings.

• **Great Smoky Mountains National Park, Tennessee/North Carolina - Alum Cave Trail to Mt. LeConte**

Distance: 11 miles (round trip).

Duration: 6–8 hours

Highlights: The Alum Cave Trail leads to Mount LeConte's top, which is a tough climb. The trail's environments are diverse, with woodland trails, rocky outcrops, and stunning vistas. Spending the night at the LeConte Lodge (reservations necessary) lets you to take in the peak views at dawn and sunset. It's an excellent way to see the Smokies in a weekend.

• **Zion National Park, Utah - Observation Point**

Distance: 8 miles (round-trip) Time: 5-7 hours

Highlights: The Observation Point Trail offers panoramic views of Zion Canyon and its surroundings. The hike requires a big rise and provides beautiful views along the way. This is an excellent weekend journey for people wishing to enjoy Zion's grandeur in a short period of time, whether camping in the park or staying in nearby hotels.

• **Yosemite National Park, California - Clouds Rest Distance: 14 miles (round-trip) Time: 6-8 hours**

Highlights: Clouds Rest provides amazing views of Yosemite Valley and Half Dome. The trail is a gradual ascent with a few exposed portions that reward hikers with stunning views. For a weekend break, camp nearby or stay at one of Yosemite's lodges. It's a difficult but achievable walk that provides an unforgettable experience in Yosemite.

Weekend vacations are an excellent opportunity to discover new routes and spend more time outdoors without committing to a full week. These treks allow you to challenge yourself while also enjoying the beauty of different environments.

Challenging Multi-Day Hikes

For those who are willing to tackle more difficult terrain and longer distances, hard multi-day walks provide an opportunity to fully immerse themselves in the nature. These walks take considerable planning and preparation, but they are extremely rewarding.

• **California's John Muir Trail connects Yosemite Valley and Mt. Whitney.**

Distance: 211 miles.

Duration: 2–4 weeks

Highlights: The John Muir Trail, which runs from Yosemite Valley to Mount Whitney, is a famous long-distance journey in the Sierra Nevada. The path runs through breathtaking scenery, including high mountain passes, alpine lakes, and deep woods. It's a difficult walk that needs much planning, but the payoff is a memorable adventure through some of California's most stunning terrain.

The Colorado Trail, from Denver to Durango.

Distance: 486 miles.

Duration: 4–6 weeks

Highlights: The Colorado Trail provides a unique hiking experience, ranging from alpine meadows to high mountain summits. The path passes across the Rocky Mountains and offers spectacular views of Colorado's diverse scenery. It's a difficult multi-day trek that necessitates careful planning and resupply tactics, but it's a worthwhile expedition for experienced hikers looking for a long-term challenge.

• **The Pacific Crest Trail spans from Northern California** to Southern Oregon in California, Oregon, and Washington states.

Distance: 266 miles.

Duration: 3–5 weeks.

Highlights: This section of the Pacific Crest Trail allows you to enjoy the various vistas of the Sierra Nevada and southern Oregon. The path features difficult climbs, gorgeous views, and diverse terrain. It's a difficult walk that needs physical preparation and careful planning, but it's a fantastic opportunity to experience some of the West's most stunning wilderness areas.

Challenging multi-day hikes challenge your endurance and determination. They provide an opportunity to fully immerse oneself in nature and get the benefits of completing a long-distance trip.

Trail Loop Options

Trail loops are ideal for intermediate hikers searching for variation and a full experience in one trek. They provide a continuous path that returns to the starting place, frequently featuring various topography and visual attractions.

• **Kings Canyon National Park, California: Mist Falls and Rae Lakes Loop (41 kilometers)**

Duration: 4–6 days

Highlights: The Mist Falls and Rae Lakes Loop combines spectacular waterfalls, alpine lakes, and huge meadows. The path offers a moderate challenge, with modest elevation increase and diverse terrain. Camping along the road allows for a multi-day journey in breathtaking landscape.

• **Lonesome Lake Trail,** New Hampshire: Loop around the lake.

Distance: 3.2 miles.

Duration: 2–3 hours

Highlights: The short circle hike provides breathtaking views of Lonesome Lake and the neighboring White Mountains. The path has some steep portions and rocky terrain, but it is suitable for intermediate hikers. The circle offers a lovely stroll with stunning lake vistas and mountain landscapes.

• **The Timberline Trail in Mt. Hood National Forest, Oregon, is 41 miles long.**

Duration: 3–5 days

Highlights: The Timberline Trail circles Mount Hood and provides a variety of landscapes, including woods, alpine meadows and glaciers. The path has numerous hard portions with elevation rises and changing weather conditions. It's an excellent choice for intermediate hikers seeking a longer, looping experience with breathtaking scenery.

Loop paths provide a sense of success when completed in a circuit and can offer a variety of experiences within a single trip. They are ideal for individuals who appreciate diversity and want to make the most of their trekking experience.

Final Thoughts

Intermediate hiking provides up a plethora of intriguing opportunities, ranging from moderate day walks to hard multi-day trips. These sample itineraries are intended to help you challenge your limits while enjoying the trip. As you go through increasingly difficult walks, you will develop confidence, endurance, and a new appreciation for nature's beauty.

Each trek provides a unique mix of experiences and rewards, so select the ones that match your interests and ability level. Remember to fully prepare, listen to your body, and enjoy every moment on the route. Happy trekking, and may your experiences continue to inspire and challenge you!

CHAPTER 8

EXAMPLE ITINERARIES

FOR ADVANCED HIKERS

For those who have perfected their hiking abilities and are ready to face more difficult terrain, advanced hiking provides a whole new level of excitement. If you're an experienced hiker eager to challenge your limitations, this chapter will show you some exciting itineraries. From strenuous day treks that test your stamina to sophisticated multi-day trips that immerse you in isolated nature, these paths are meant to both challenge and inspire. We'll also look at several excellent backpacking routes and long-distance paths that provide an unforgettable hiking experience.

Difficult Day Hikes

Difficult day treks are ideal for days when you want to push yourself to the maximum but still want to come home in the evening. These climbs frequently include steep ascents, difficult terrain, and large height gains, but the scenery and sense of success are well worth the effort.

• **Half Dome at Yosemite National Park, California.**

Distance: 14-16 miles (round-trip) Time: 10-12 hours

Highlights: The Half Dome trek is one of the most famous and challenging day hikes in the United States. It features a difficult ascent with the iconic cable part near the peak. The views from the summit are stunning, offering sweeping panoramas of Yosemite Valley, the High Sierra, and beyond. This hike needs a permit, so plan early and get ready for a physically tough trip.

Tuckerman Ravine Trail on Mount Washington, New Hampshire.

Distance: 8.2 miles (round-trip) Time: 6-8 hours

Highlights: Known for its changeable weather and rough terrain, Mount Washington is a tough trek with breathtaking views. The Tuckerman Ravine Trail is steep and arduous, climbing through alpine terrain to the peak. On clear days, the views are stunning, with a panoramic panorama of the White Mountains and beyond. Be prepared for shifting weather and strong winds.

• **The Enchantments, Washington - Core Loop.**

Distance: 18 miles.

Duration: 8–10 hours

Highlights: The Core Enchantments Loop has breathtaking alpine landscapes, such as crystal-clear lakes, granite peaks, and wildflower-filled meadows. This trek has substantial elevation gain and rough terrain, making it a challenging yet rewarding trip. The route leads past a series of gorgeous lakes, each one more magnificent than the previous. Permits are necessary, so plan accordingly.

Difficult day hikes are an excellent opportunity to push yourself while also getting the satisfaction of finishing a tough walk in a single day. These walks have a combination of technical obstacles and beautiful vistas, making them perfect for experienced hikers seeking a day-long adventure.

Advanced Multi-Day Expeditions

Advanced multi-day adventures transport you deep into distant wilderness locations, allowing you to enjoy nature's raw splendor. These hikes need meticulous preparation, physical stamina, and self-reliance.

• **The Haute Route in France/Switzerland.**

Distance: 120 miles.

Duration: 12–14 days

Highlights: The Haute Route is a famous high-altitude journey over the French and Swiss Alps. The path passes through magnificent mountain scenery, including glaciers, alpine meadows, and craggy summits. It's a strenuous trek with steep elevation changes and difficult terrain. The hike includes staying in mountain huts or campsites and necessitates a high degree of fitness and planning.

• **The Wonderland Trail at Mount Rainier National Park, Washington.**

Distance: 93 miles.

Duration: 9–11 days

Highlights: The Wonderland Trail circles Mount Rainier, offering a full overview of the mountain's various environments. The walk passes through lush woods, alpine meadows, and glacial streams, with spectacular views of the renowned peak. The trek has large elevation climbs and unpredictable weather situations. Backpacking permits are necessary, and hikers should be ready for a variety of circumstances.

• **The Lost Coast Trail in California.**

Distance: 25 miles.

Duration: 3–4 days

Highlights: The Lost Coast Trail is a wild and rough coastline trail in northern California. It has breathtaking ocean vistas, quiet beaches, and tough terrain. The path entails crossing tidal zones and passing through tough, unlabeled areas. It's a really wild experience, with few facilities and restricted access, perfect for experienced explorers looking for a distant and hard journey.

Advanced multi-day adventures allow you to immerse yourself in some of the most beautiful and inaccessible regions on the world. These climbs need a high degree of physical endurance, self-reliance, and meticulous planning, but the benefits far outweigh the effort.

Backpacking Routes

Backpacking routes mix the difficulty of long-distance trekking with the excitement of sleeping out in nature. These routes allow you to explore different terrains and spend more time in nature.

• **The Long Trail in Vermont.**

Distance: 273 miles.

Duration: 3–4 weeks

Highlights: The Long path is the oldest long-distance path in the United States, stretching the length of Vermont from Massachusetts to Canada. The path combines difficult terrain, alpine panoramas, and lush woodlands. It's a strenuous walk with multiple steep portions and harsh weather. The path gives a thorough experience of Vermont's wilderness and includes a variety of shelters and campsites along the way.

- **The Continental Divide Trail in New Mexico's Gila Wilderness**

Distance: 100 miles (segment).

Duration: 7–10 days

Highlights: The Gila Wilderness part of the Continental Divide Trail combines steep mountains, arid gorges, and lush woods. The path includes hot springs, secluded wilderness locations, and diverse terrain. It's a difficult route with limited conveniences that necessitates meticulous preparation for hydration and replenishment.

- **The Wonderland Trail at Mount Rainier National Park, Washington.**

Distance: 93 miles.

Duration: 7–10 days

Highlights: The Wonderland Trail provides a thorough backpacking experience around Mount Rainier. The path offers a variety of landscapes, including glaciers, alpine meadows, and old-growth woods. It's a strenuous hike with substantial elevation increase and changing weather conditions. Permits and meticulous planning are required for the trip, which includes food and water resupplies.

Backpacking routes allow you to experience the nature in a more immersive way by mixing long-distance trekking with camping and self-reliance. These routes test your endurance and let you to explore some of the most isolated and picturesque locations.

Long-distance trails

Long-distance routes are the ultimate test of hiking endurance and determination. These itineraries cover hundreds of kilometers and provide opportunities to explore various landscapes and isolated wilderness locations.

• **The Appalachian Trail spans 2,193 miles in the eastern United States.**

Duration: 5-7 months (through trek).

Highlights: The Appalachian Trail runs from Georgia to Maine, spanning 14 states and presenting a wide variety of vistas, from southern woodlands to New England highlands. Thru-hiking the AT is a significant feat that requires months of planning and physical stamina. The path travels through numerous national parks and wilderness regions, giving a complete view of the eastern United States wilderness.

- **Pacific Crest Trail, Western U.S.**

Distance: 2,650 miles.

Duration: 4 to 6 months (through-hike)

Highlights: The Pacific Crest Trail spans from Mexico to Canada through California, Oregon, and Washington. The path crosses deserts, mountains, and woods. It's a strenuous hike that demands cautious preparation, replenishment, and stamina. The PCT provides breathtaking vistas of the Sierra Nevada and Cascade Ranges, making it an ideal long-distance hiking destination.

- **The Te Araroa Trail in New Zealand.**

Distance: 1,864 miles.

Duration: 3 to 5 months (through-hike)

Highlights: The Te Araroa Trail connects New Zealand's north and south islands. The path features a variety of sceneries, including beaches, mountains, and woods. It's a strenuous trek with varying terrain and weather situations that offers a thorough view of New Zealand's natural splendor.

Long-distance routes are the pinnacle of hiking experiences, allowing you to immerse yourself in the woods and test your stamina over long miles. These paths demand extensive preparation, including physical training, logistical planning, and resupply tactics.

Final Thoughts

Advanced hiking is not for the faint-hearted. It requires physical stamina, mental endurance, and rigorous planning. However, the benefits are enormous: stunning vistas, remote wilderness encounters, and the exhilaration of pushing your limitations. Whether you're taking on demanding day walks, complex multi-day trips, backpacking routes, or long-distance trails, each experience provides its own set of difficulties and rewards.

As you prepare for these advanced climbs, remember to bring the proper equipment, plan ahead of time, and be aware of the conditions and your own physical limitations. With the proper planning and perspective, these difficult routes will give some of the most memorable and gratifying experiences of your hiking trip.

CHAPTER 9

TOP HIKING TRAILS IN

MISSOURI

If you enjoy hiking and want to discover Missouri's natural splendor, you're in for a treat. The state has a diverse network of trails, each with its own set of scenery and experiences. Missouri's hiking paths accommodate hikers of all skill levels, from rocky hills and picturesque overlooks to quiet river valleys and lush woodlands. In this chapter, I'll walk you through some of the best trails in the state, each with its own unique beauty and challenge.

Ozark Trail

The Ozark Trail is a hidden treasure in Missouri's hiking scene. It is one of the state's longest and most diversified routes, spanning more than 350 miles. This walk has lush forests, undulating hills, magnificent river vistas, and difficult terrain. It's a path that takes time and effort but pays with some of the greatest hiking experiences Missouri has to offer.

- **The Ozark Trail connects the St. Francois Mountains** and Mark Twain National Forest via the Ozark National Scenic Riverways. The path is separated into parts, each providing unique experiences and difficulties. You may trek a single part or the full path for an authentic backcountry experience.

- **Key sections:**

Courtois brook is recognized for its picturesque brook crossings and rich woodlands. It's quite easy, making it an excellent beginning to the Ozark Trail.

The Taum Sauk section of the route has harsh terrain with steep hills and rough roads. The views from this area are magnificent.

The Eleven Point Section provides stunning river vistas and a more distant hiking experience. It's ideal for individuals who want to get away from the throng and spend some time alone.

• **The Ozark Trail boasts various landscapes,** including breathtaking vistas from the Berryman Trail and tranquil serenity along the Current River. The trail's length allows you to adjust your trip to your schedule and ability level, making it a versatile option for hikers of all levels.

Hiking the Ozark Trail is like exploring Missouri's natural history. Whether you're searching for a day trek or a multi-day expedition, this path offers a diverse and enjoyable experience.

Taum Sauk Mountain Trail

The Taum Sauk Mountain Trail is a must-see if you want to experience stunning views and a hard trek. Taum Sauk Mountain, Missouri's highest peak, provides breathtaking panoramic vistas and a difficult walk that is well worth it.

• **The Taum Sauk Mountain Trail is part of Taum Sauk Mountain State Park,** recognized for its difficult terrain and high elevation. The path is an 8.2-mile loop with an elevation increase of roughly 1,500 feet. It's a strenuous trek with some of the nicest vistas in the state.

• **Highlights:**

The route offers spectacular vistas, including the classic panorama from the top of Taum Sauk Mountain. On a clear day, you can see for kilometers, with views that extend across the Ozark Plateau.

Hikers will find remarkable rock formations, such as the magnificent Devil's Tollgate. These formations lend a geological depth to the climb, making it more visually appealing.

The walk goes near multiple waterfalls, including the scenic Mina Sauk Falls. It's a terrific place to relax and appreciate the beauty of falling water.

• **Trail Experience:** The Taum Sauk Mountain Trail is noted for its challenging and rocky terrain. It has some difficult ascents that need appropriate hiking footwear and physical stamina. However, the exertion is rewarded with stunning vistas and a fulfilling sense of accomplishment.

The Taum Sauk Mountain Trail is suitable for hikers searching for a hard climb with rewarding results. It's an opportunity to visit Missouri's highest peak while also enjoying some of the state's most magnificent landscape.

Bell Mountain Trail

Bell Mountain Trail provides a more quiet and serene hiking experience, with breathtaking vistas and a diverse terrain. It's an excellent choice for anyone want to see Missouri's natural beauty without the crowds.

• **The Bell Mountain Trail, located in the Mark Twain National Forest,** is roughly 10 miles long. It is noted for its harsh landscape, which includes steep slopes and rocky areas. The path offers spectacular views of the neighboring Ozarks and is popular among experienced hikers.

• **Highlights:**

The peak of Bell Mountain provides panoramic views of the surrounding area. It's a terrific place to relax and enjoy the splendor of the Ozark Mountains.

The path offers diverse terrain, including wooded parts, rocky outcrops, and wide meadows. This type provides a fascinating and diverse hiking experience.

The route offers excellent wildlife watching opportunities, including deer, turkey, and other bird species. The trail's peaceful and secluded location makes it perfect for seeing animals in its natural environment.

• **The Bell Mountain Trail has tough aspects,** such as steep climbs and rocky ground. It's best suited for hikers who enjoy rough terrain and prefer a more alone experience.

Bell Mountain Trail is ideal for people who want a more distant and tranquil hiking experience. With its difficult terrain and breathtaking vistas, it's a rewarding excursion for experienced hikers.

Powdermill Trail

Powder Mill Trail provides a unique hiking experience along the Current River, complete with stunning river vistas and a variety of natural elements. It's a wonderful alternative for someone who enjoys both trekking and river sports.

• **The Powder Mill Trail,** part of the Ozark National Scenic Riverways, is approximately 4 miles long. The route follows the Current River and provides a moderately simple trek with scenic views of the river and surrounding woodland.

• **Highlights:**

The walk offers spectacular views of the Current River, with various areas to enjoy the tranquil landscape. It's an ideal location for photography and leisure.

The path passes near historical structures, such as the old Powder Mill, adding historical importance to the trek.

The route provides possibilities for animal observation and exploring the rich flora of the Ozarks. Keep a look out for deer, birds, and other plant species.

• **The Powder Mill Trail is accessible** to hikers of all experience levels due to its relative ease. It's an excellent choice for a relaxing day stroll with stunning river views and the opportunity to learn about the area's natural and historical features.

Powder Mill Trail is great for people searching for a gorgeous yet simple trek. With its river vistas and historical characteristics, it provides a peaceful and pleasurable hiking experience.

Current River Trail

The Current River Trail is a classic trek that highlights the beauty of one of Missouri's most recognizable rivers. It's a diverse path with both hard and picturesque portions.

• **The Current River Trail is roughly** 10 miles long and runs through the Ozark National Scenic Riverways. The path crosses a variety of terrains, including riverbanks, woodlands, and rocky outcrops.

• **Highlights:**

The route has many access spots to the Current River, ideal for activities like fishing, swimming, and resting.

The walk offers scenic views of the river and surrounding scenery. Along the journey, you will see gorgeous views and stunning river bends.

The walk includes remarkable geological structures such as caverns and rock outcrops. These elements provide a distinct character to the trek and are ideal for investigation.

• **The Current River Trail has a combination** of easy and challenging parts, including some rocky and uneven terrain. It's an excellent choice for hikers seeking a balance of rest and excitement.

The Current River Trail combines visual beauty with outdoor recreation. It's an excellent alternative for individuals who want to appreciate the beauty of the Current River while also having a variety trekking experience.

Hawn State Park Trails

Hawn State Park, located in the Ozarks, is a refuge for wildlife aficionados. The park, which spans over 5,000 acres, includes both calm woodland walks and stunning rock formations.

The Pickle Creek Trail is an easy trek with stunning scenery. This 3.5-mile circle follows the flowing Pickle Creek, providing peaceful woodland vistas and occasional glimpses of animals. The creek gives a calm element to the trip, and the route is especially lovely in spring when wildflowers blossom.

• **The Rock Garden Trail,** a 3.3-mile circle over steep terrain, offers a more challenging hike. This walk leads you through a landscape filled with intriguing rock formations and includes some steep portions. The exertion is rewarded with breathtaking vistas and a sense of satisfaction as you cross rocky rocks.

• **White Rock Mountain Trail:** A challenging 5-mile walk for experienced hikers. It's a hard trek with steep ascents and rocky trails, but the panoramic views from the top of White Rock Mountain make it worthwhile. On a clear day, you can see for miles across the Ozarks, providing for an unforgettable hiking experience.

Highlights: Hawn State Park is known for its beautiful beauty and diverse topography. The combination of easy and difficult walks makes it a flexible location. Don't pass up the opportunity to appreciate Pickle Creek's calm surroundings and the raw beauty of the Rock Garden.

Rockwoods Reservation Trails

Rock woods Reservation, a short drive from St. Louis, provides an accessible getaway into nature. This 1,880-acre reserve has a broad mix of paths suitable for all ability levels.

• **The Rock Quarry Trail is a 4.2-mile circle across tough terrain,** passing via an ancient rock quarry. The trail's rough portions and steep climbs make it relatively difficult, but the diverse terrain, which includes stunning overlooks and deep woodland, makes the trek fascinating.

• **The Goat Cliff Trail,** at 2.2 miles, is a shorter and more challenging trek. The trail's centerpiece is Goat Cliff, which offers panoramic views of the surrounding region. The hike to the peak is difficult and rocky, but the view is well worth it.

• **Wildcat Trail:** A 3.5-mile circle with woodland and grassland scenery. The Wildcat Trail is somewhat challenging, with some pleasant climbs and descents. It's an excellent choice if you're seeking for a peaceful trek with the opportunity to see local animals.

Highlights: The Rock woods Reservation is known for its diverse terrain, which ranges from rocky outcrops to tranquil meadows. The paths here have something for everyone, whether you're looking for a difficult climb or a relaxing walk.

Castlewood State Park Trails

Castlewood State Park is famous for its magnificent river vistas and rocky terrain. The park's paths run along the Meramec River and provide a diversified hiking experience.

• **The Lone Wolf Trail** is a 3.5-mile circle through lush woodland and along the Meramec River. This fairly hard hike has several steep portions and rough terrain. The reward is a stunning combination of river vistas and woodland scenery, with several possibilities to see wildlife.

• **The River Scene Trail** is a 2.8-mile circle with convenient access to the Meramec River, ideal for a relaxing trek. The route is reasonably flat and ideal for a leisurely stroll, with several opportunities to admire the river's tranquil beauty.

• **The Castlewood Trail is a 7-mile loop offering** a more challenging hiking experience. It has some steep climbs and rocky areas, but the vistas of the Meramec River and surrounding environment are stunning. It's a satisfying trek for anyone wishing to push themselves while admiring the scenery.

Castlewood State Park is recognized for its stunning river vistas and diversified topography. The park's routes range from simple to difficult, with something for every hiker. The picturesque grandeur of the Meramec River lends a unique dimension to your hiking adventure.

Washington State Park Trails

Washington State Park, located in eastern Missouri, has a variety of paths that showcase the area's natural splendor. The park's 7,500 acres contain wooded regions, hills, and fascinating geological formations.

- **The Rocky Ridge Trail is a 4.2-mile circle** across tough terrain with stunning vistas from its high points. The track has steep slopes and rough sections, making it a difficult trek. The panoramic vistas of the surrounding environment are a real feature.

- **The Taum Sauk Trail is a 3.6-mile circle** that leads to stunning views of the park. The Taum Sauk Trail is quite tough and alternates between wooded and open grassland portions. It's an excellent choice if you want a trek that mixes beauty and hardship.

- **The Buzzard's Roost Trail, a 2.5-mile trek,** leads to a high vantage point with panoramic views of the area. Although the route has some steep and rocky portions, the view from the summit is well worth it.

Highlights: Washington State Park has a variety of routes via stunning bluffs and difficult terrain. The trails here are noted for their natural beauty and tough parts, making it an excellent choice for anyone wishing to explore Missouri's different landscapes.

Katy Trail State Park

The Katy Trail State Park is one of Missouri's best long-distance paths. It spans 237 miles and follows the route of the former Missouri-Kansas-Texas (MKT) Railroad, providing a flat, easy climb with stunning vistas.

• **From St. Charles to Hermann,** the Katy Trail offers breathtaking vistas of the Missouri River and lovely tiny villages. Hermann, noted for its wines and historical buildings, is a worthwhile trip. This segment is suitable for hikers of all skill levels because to its flat and easy terrain.

• **From Hermann to Rocheport,** the walk offers spectacular river views and goes through the historic town. The level, well-maintained route is ideal for a leisurely trek or bike ride, with lots of opportunity to admire the scenery.

• **The Katy Trail connects Rocheport to Clinton,** passing through agricultural and forested regions. It's a lengthier stretch, but it offers a thorough overview of the trail's splendor. The flat terrain makes it ideal for multi-day treks or bike journeys.

Highlights: Katy Trail State Park is known for its scenic beauty and historical significance. The route is a flat, easy stroll that provides wonderful vistas of the Missouri River and pleasant tiny villages. It's a great choice for both day walks and larger multi-day trips.

These best Missouri trails provide a wide range of hiking experiences, from peaceful river walks to strenuous climbs with panoramic vistas. Each route has its own distinct appeal, making it worthwhile to explore them all. Whether you choose a simple trek or a more challenging excursion, Missouri's trails have something for everyone. So lace up your boots, grab your kit, and hit the trail; Missouri's natural splendor is waiting to be discovered.

CHAPTER 10

TRAIL REVIEW AND HIGHLIGHTS

As an experienced hiker who has traveled many of Missouri's trails, I understand that each path provides a unique trip. In this chapter, I'll lead you through extensive descriptions of some of the most popular trails, highlighting their gorgeous vistas and distinctive characteristics, as well as providing trail ratings and suggestions. Whether you're a beginner or an experienced hiker, knowing what each path has to offer might help you plan your next outdoor adventure.

Detailed Reviews of Popular Trails

Missouri is endowed with a diverse range of hiking routes that appeal to all types of hikers. Here are some detailed descriptions of popular routes that highlight the state's different landscapes:

1. Ozark Trail overview: The Ozark Trail runs over 200 miles through the Ozark National Scenic Riverways and the Mark Twain National Forest. It is a long-distance path that provides a deep dive into Missouri's harsh and picturesque landscape.

Highlights: • The path features different sceneries such as lush forests, rocky slopes, and undulating hills. Expect a combination of nice pathways and difficult rocky terrain.

• **The Ozark Trail offers stunning vistas** from its high spots. You'll find breathtaking overlooks with wide views of the Ozark Mountains and the meandering rivers below.

• **The route is home to a variety of species,** including deer, wild turkey, and the rare black bear. Birdwatchers will appreciate seeing a variety of species during the trek.

Difficulty varies based on the segment. Some sections of the path may be fairly difficult, with steep hills and rough terrain.

Recommendation: This trek is best for experienced hikers seeking a multi-day excursion. The variety of scenery and opportunities to explore Missouri's natural beauty make for a rewarding journey.

2. Taum Sauk Mountain Trail: Located in Missouri's St. Francois Mountains, this trail has the state's highest peak. The route is approximately 3.5 miles round-trip and is popular among local hikers.

Highlights: • The path features hard ascents and descents, particularly near the peak. The trail is well-marked, but be prepared for a workout.

• **At the summit,** enjoy panoramic views of the surrounding mountains and valleys. On a clear day, the panorama spans for miles, providing a spectacular perspective of the Ozarks.

• **The trail's magnificent rock** formations and boulder fields contribute to its rustic beauty.

Difficulty: Moderate to difficult due to elevation climb and rough terrain.

Recommendation: Ideal for those seeking a reasonably quick trek with a substantial result. The views from the peak are stunning and well worth the effort.

3. Overview: The Bell Mountain Trail is a 7-mile circle in the St. Francois Mountains, near Taum Sauk. This path is noted for its breathtaking landscape and difficult terrain.

Highlights: • The trek features steep ascents, rocky roads, and lush forests. It's a hard hike, but doable for those in decent shape.

• **Bell Mountain's** high spots provide panoramic views of the surrounding wooded hills and valleys.

• The trail's unique features include jagged rock formations and natural beauty. The rocky outcrops offer fantastic photo possibilities as well as a glimpse into the Ozarks' raw beauty.

Difficulty: Challenging due to high hills and rough terrain.

Recommendation: Ideal for hikers looking for a more challenging experience with wonderful vistas. The difficult terrain and breathtaking splendor make it a popular destination for anyone eager to challenge their boundaries.

4. Current River Trail Overview: The trail follows the picturesque Current River in the Ozark National picturesque Riverways. It's a simple trek with stunning views of the river and the surrounding landscape.

Highlights: • The path is largely flat with modest gradients, making it suitable for hikers of all skill levels. The trail is well-maintained and simple to navigate.

• **Enjoy scenic vistas of rivers, woods,** and wildlife. The route offers a tranquil and scenic backdrop for a leisurely trek.

• **Unique Features:** The trail's proximity to the river allows for water-based activities such as fishing and kayaking.

Difficulty: Easy to moderate. Suitable for all ability levels, including families and new hikers.

Recommendation: Ideal for a peaceful day trek or family outing. The picturesque splendor and simple topography make it ideal for a relaxing hike.

Scenic Views and Unique Features

Missouri's trails are all distinct in terms of beauty and characteristics. Here's a deeper look at what distinguishes these trails:

1. Ozark Trail • Scenic Views: The high overlooks along the Ozark Trail provide some of the nicest views in Missouri. The vistas of the Ozark Mountains and the flowing rivers below are magnificent.

• Unique Features: The trail's variety is one of its most distinctive features. The various vistas, which range from deep woods to steep hills and river valleys, make the trek intriguing.

2. Taum Sauk Mountain Trail: • The peak offers stunning panoramic views. A clear day allows you to view for miles, taking in the Ozarks' rolling hills and wide woodlands.

• Unique features: Hiking to Missouri's highest peak provides a sense of accomplishment. The rock formations and boulder fields are additional prominent characteristics that contribute to the trail's raw attractiveness.

3. Bell Mountain Trail • Scenic Views: The high spots of Bell Mountain provide amazing views of the surrounding area. The mix of jagged rock formations and broad woodland vistas results in a visually stunning experience.

- **The trail's tough topography and rock formations** provide a sense of adventure. The harsh topography and natural beauty combine for an unforgettable walk.

4. Current River walk • Scenic Views: The walk offers stunning views of the Current River, rich woodlands, and occasional wildlife sightings.

- **Unique Features:** The trail's availability to aquatic activities enhances the trekking experience. The river location creates a tranquil and attractive backdrop.

Trail Ratings and Recommendations

Choosing the proper path is determined by your skill level, interests, and desired experience. Here's an overview of trail ratings and suggestions based on several criteria:

1. Ozark Trail

- **Rating:** 4.5/5

• **Recommendation:** Ideal for experienced hikers seeking a multi-day journey. The various terrain and spectacular sights make it an excellent choice for anyone seeking a challenge.

2. Taum Sauk Mountain Trail

- **Rating:** 4/5

- **Recommendation:** Suitable for hikers wanting a short yet satisfying ascent. The vistas from the peak are well worth the effort, making this an excellent day trip.

3. Bell Mountain Trail

- **Rating:** 4.5/5

- **Recommendation:** Ideal for hikers seeking a difficult journey with wonderful vistas. The steep terrain and spectacular vistas make for an unforgettable journey.

4. Current River Trail

- **Rating**: 4/5

- **Recommendation:** Suitable for families, novices, and leisurely hikers. The simple topography and gorgeous river views make it an ideal location for a peaceful excursion.

Each of these paths provides a distinct hiking experience, ranging from strenuous climbs to relaxing river walks. Understanding the features of each route might help you select the best trek for your ability level and interests.

Whether you're looking for stunning views, challenging terrain, or a peaceful respite, Missouri's trails have something for you. So, lace up your boots, pack your stuff, and hit the road; adventure awaits!

CHAPTER 11

EXPLORING MISSOURI'S
NATURAL BEAUTY

Hiking across Missouri is like entering a live, breathing canvas of natural beauty. Missouri has a tremendous variety of flora and wildlife, hidden jewels, and magnificent locations, ranging from the lush Ozark forests to the gorgeous river valleys. This chapter will delve into Missouri's rich ecosystems, highlight some of its most stunning and lesser-known gems, and provide techniques for capturing the beauty of your experiences via photography.

Flora and Fauna of Missouri

Missouri's natural environments are filled with various plant and animal life. Understanding the flora and fauna may improve your hiking experience, making each trip not only a physical excursion but also an immersing exploration of the state's natural heritage.

Flora

1. Missouri's woods are largely oak-hickory woodlands, with oak and hickory trees as the dominant species. The Ozarks include a diverse range of hardwoods, including maple, beech, and elm. As you trek through these forests, the towering trees and deep canopy provide a peaceful and pleasant atmosphere. In the spring and summer, look for wildflowers such as the colorful trillium and the delicate bluebell poking through the underbrush.

2. Prairies: The western half of the state is characterized by vast plains that were once dominated by tall grasses and wildflowers. Common plants are the purple coneflower and the vivid yellow black-eyed Susan. These plains, with their wide vistas and vibrant wildflower displays, provide a unique type of beauty.

3. Wetlands and Riverbanks: Missouri's wetlands and riverbanks support a diverse range of plant species, including sedges, rushes, and willows. Along the Current River, for example, you may encounter luxuriant riverine flora that flourishes in the damp, fertile soil.

Fauna

1. Animals: Missouri's woodlands and plains are home to a diverse range of animals. White-tailed deer are frequently sighted feeding in open fields or traveling through the forests. The region also has coyotes and bobcats, though they are more elusive. In the marshes, you could see a river otter, which is noted for its lively behavior.

2. Birds: Missouri is a birdwatcher's heaven. The state is home to a diverse assortment of bird species, including the magnificent bald eagle flying above the river valleys and the bright eastern bluebird. In the spring and summer, the woods are alive with warbler songs and woodpecker sounds.

3. Reptiles and Amphibians: Missouri's diversified ecosystems support a wide variety of reptiles and amphibians. The Eastern box turtle is prevalent in the forests, while the wetlands are home to species such as the

American toad and the green tree frog. On a warm day, you may hear a bullfrog's unique croak along the water's edge.

4. Insects: The state's diverse habitats support a wide range of insects, including butterflies such as the Eastern tiger swallowtail and dragonflies that dart over ponds. In the plains, bees pollinate wildflowers and insects among the tall grasses.

Scenic and Hidden Gems

Missouri is full with well-known gorgeous sites, but there are also lots of hidden gems that provide a more private experience. Here's a look at some of the state's most scenic spots, including both iconic and lesser-known jewels.

1. Elephant Rocks State Park.

Overview: Elephant Rocks State Park, located in the St. Francois Mountains, is well-known for its gigantic granite rocks that resemble an elephant herd. The park's primary walk, the Braille walk, is a brief yet intriguing stroll amid these massive stones.

Highlights: The view of these massive rocks against the backdrop of the surrounding forest is simply breathtaking.

The park also provides a panoramic view from a high elevation, which is ideal for seeing a sunset.

Hidden Gem: If you wander off the main track, you can come upon smaller, less-visited boulders and rock formations. These provide unusual vistas and excellent photographic opportunity.

2. Meramec Caverns Overview: The Meramec Caverns near Stanton provide a unique subterranean experience. These limestone caverns have spectacular stalactites and stalagmites, as well as unusual formations such as "Aladdin's Castle."

Highlights: Guided excursions through several chambers provide insight into the cave's geological history. The illumination in the tunnels highlights the majestic aspect of the rock formations.

Hidden Gem: The less-touristy portions of the caverns, which are occasionally included in special excursions, offer a more intimate view of the cave's natural characteristics.

3. Johnson's Shut-Ins State Park Overview: Johnson's Shut-Ins is known for its stunning rock formations and the Black River's carvings through ancient granite. The park's name refers to the natural "shut-ins" in which the river is driven through tight openings in the rock.

Highlights: The shut-ins produce natural pools and waterfalls, making this a popular swimming and picnic area. The sights of the river snaking through the rugged scenery are simply breathtaking.

Hidden Gem: Look for less-trafficked routes with more quiet river views and shut-ins. These locations offer a more relaxing experience away from the major park areas.

4. Castlewood State Park Overview: Castlewood State Park, located along the Meramec River, provides scenic vistas, wooded paths, and steep terrain. The park's routes range from moderate walks to strenuous treks.

Highlights: The river view is stunning, particularly from the path overlooks. The park's pathways provide a variety of viewpoints on the area, ranging from gorgeous river vistas to deep forests.

Hidden Gem: Lesser-known routes, such as the less-hiked parts of the River Scene Trail, provide a more quiet experience with less people.

Photography Advice for Hikers

Photographing the natural beauty of Missouri's trails may be quite rewarding. Here are some ideas to help you take the greatest photographs when hiking:

1. Plan your shots.

Before you go out, investigate the terrain and prepare your shots. Look for certain aspects or angles that you wish to capture. Understanding the trail's highlights and potential problems will allow you to arrange the optimal times to photograph.

2. Use natural light.

The finest light for photography is usually found during the golden hours—early morning or late afternoon. The soft, warm light at these times may bring out the colors and textures in your images. Avoid photography in the bright noon sun, which can result in sharp shadows and overexposed highlights.

3. Frame your shots.

Use the natural environment to frame your photographs. Trees, rocks, and other natural objects may act as frames or foregrounds in your photographs, adding depth to them. Pay attention to the composition and employ leading lines to attract the viewer's gaze into the image.

4. Capture Details

Don't forget to photograph the little elements of nature. Close-ups of wildflowers, tree bark textures, and the play of light on leaves may all give a unique viewpoint on the trail's beauty. A macro lens can be especially beneficial in this style of photography.

5. Stay steady.

Hiking sometimes entails uneven terrain, making it difficult to keep your camera steady. If feasible, use a tripod, especially in low light or for longer exposures. If a tripod isn't an option, support yourself against a solid surface or utilize the camera's image stabilization functions.

6. Respect the environment.

While it may be tempting to get the ideal photo, remember to respect the surroundings. Stick to the established pathways and prevent trampling on fragile plants. Leave no trace and make sure your presence does not detract from the natural beauty you are recording.

7. Experiment with angles

Don't be scared to try new angles and views. Get low to the earth for a new perspective, or photograph from higher elevations to capture broad views. Sometimes the most beautiful images are taken from unexpected perspectives.

8. Post-processing

After your trek, spend some time editing your images to improve the quality. Make your photographs stand out by adjusting their brightness, contrast, and hues. However, be careful not to over-edit your images, since you want them to capture the actual beauty of the path.

Exploring Missouri's natural beauties is a journey of discovery, complete with diverse flora and wildlife, breathtaking scenery, and hidden gems. Whether you're trekking through lush forests, along gorgeous riverbanks, or exploring unusual geological formations, each path has its own set of surprises. Understanding the state's natural ecosystems, uncovering lesser-known jewels, and documenting its beauty via smart photography will allow you to completely enjoy and share the great experiences that Missouri's trails have to provide. So take your camera, hit the trails, and let the adventure begin—Missouri's natural splendor is waiting for you to discover and photograph.

CHAPTER 12

SEASONAL HIKING

CONSIDERATIONS

Hiking in Missouri is a year-round activity, with each season offering its own set of difficulties and pleasures. As a seasoned hiker, I've seen the beauty and difficulty of the paths in every season. Understanding the differences between seasons might help you plan your hikes more effectively and make the most of them. In this chapter, we'll look at what you need to know about hiking in spring, summer, fall, and winter to be safe and enjoy the finest of Missouri's trails all year.

Spring Hiking Tips

Spring is a great season for trekking. The environment comes alive as plants blossom and animals awaken from their winter hibernation. However, it is also a season that need cautious planning owing to fluctuating weather and trail conditions.

1. Weather and Gear.

Springtime weather in Missouri may be unpredictable. You can get a combination of sunny days, rain showers, and the odd cool breeze. It is critical to be prepared for such swings.

• **Dress in layers to adapt to changing temperatures.** Begin with a moisture-wicking base layer to keep perspiration off your skin, then add an insulating layer for warmth, and finish with a waterproof and windproof jacket. This allows you to alter your attire as needed during the day.

• **Recommended footwear**: Waterproof hiking boots for muddy and wet trails during spring rains. Make sure they have enough traction to handle slippery weather.

2. Trail conditions.

Spring thaw can result in muddy and uneven path conditions. Be ready for:

• **To avoid mud and puddles,** use waterproof boots and gaiters. Stick to existing paths to prevent hurting the surrounding plants and reducing your influence on the trail.

• **Stream Crossings:** Heavy rains and melting snow can cause overflowing streams or creeks on certain paths. Be cautious when crossing water, and consider utilizing trekking poles for support.

3. Wildlife and Flora.

Spring is an excellent time to see animals and appreciate the abundant plant life.

• **Wild flowers:** Early bloomers include trilliums, Virginia bluebells, and dogwood blooms. These flowers offer a pop of color to the scene and may be found in a variety of woodlands and meadows.

• **Wildlife:** Deer and wild turkeys become more active. Keep an eye out for them and listen for returning birds' songs, such as robins and warblers.

4. Safety considerations.

• **Allergies:** Spring pollen might cause allergies. Carry medicine as required, and if pollen levels are high, consider wearing a buff or mask to protect your face.

• **Prepare for spring storms to arrive swiftly.** Check the weather forecast before going out, and be prepared to shorten your trek if necessary.

Summer Hiking Essentials

Summer in Missouri may be hot and humid, posing unique challenges compared to the other seasons. Here's how to be comfortable and safe on your summer excursions.

1. Hydration & Nutrition

Staying hydrated is essential on hot summer walks.

• **Bring enough water**—at least 2 liters per person—for a half-day trek. When hiking in places with natural water sources, bring a hydration reservoir or water bottles, as well as a water filter or purification tablets. Pack lightweight, high-energy foods like trail mix, granola bars, and fresh fruit.

These will help you maintain your energy levels without adding unnecessary weight to your bag.

2. Clothing and Sun Protection.

In the hot summer months, proper clothes and sun protection are crucial.

• **Choose lightweight,** moisture-wicking, and breathable apparel. Long sleeves and pants can shield you from the sun and insects while keeping you cool. Light colors are preferred because they reflect heat more effectively than dark ones.

• **For sun protection,** use high-SPF sunscreen, a brimmed hat, and UV-protective eyewear. Reapply sunscreen every two hours, especially if you are exercising or swimming.

3. Trail conditions.

Summer may bring both dry conditions and thunderstorms.

• **Avoid peak heat** by starting hikes early in the morning or late in the evening. Take regular rests in the shade to cool down and relax.

• **Thunderstorms** are frequently seen throughout the afternoon. Follow weather forecasts and avoid trekking during storms. If you become trapped in a storm, find cover in a low place away from trees and avoid metal things.

4. Wildlife & Flora

Summer is a period for development and activity in Missouri's wildlands.

• **Be wary of potential** contacts with wildlife, including snakes, ticks, and mosquitoes. To avoid mosquitos and ticks, use insect repellent and check for ticks after your hike.

• **Summer brings** a high prevalence of poison ivy. Learn to recognize it—its leaves are usually in clusters of three—and avoid touch to avoid skin discomfort.

Fall Hiking Highlights

Autumn is possibly the most attractive season for hiking in Missouri. The colder temps and bright fall hues create a magnificent setting.

1. Weather and Gear: Autumn weather is typically pleasant, but can range from warm days to cold evenings.

• **Dress in layers** like you would on a spring hike. Begin with a base layer, then add an insulating layer before bringing a windproof or water-resistant jacket for chilly weather.

• **Footwear:** As the leaves fall, pathways may become treacherous. Make sure your hiking boots have enough grip to traverse falling leaves and probable mud.

2. Scenic Beauty

Autumn provides some of the most breathtaking hiking opportunities in Missouri.

• **Fall Foliage:** The shifting leaf hues are a highlight. Trails such as the Ozark Trail and those in Shawnee National Forest provide stunning views of brilliant reds, oranges, and yellow.

• **The mellow,** golden light of autumn is ideal for photography. Capture the contrast between the brightly colored foliage and the beautiful blue sky.

3. Trail conditions.

Cooler weather and fallen leaves may also have an impact on trail conditions.

• **Leaves can conceal rocks and uneven ground,** despite their attractive appearance. Be wary about sliding and keep your footing.

• The weather in autumn might be unexpected. Be prepared for unexpected temperature swings and possible rain showers. Check the weather prediction and pack appropriately.

4. Wildlife & Flora

Autumn marks a transitional period for both wildlife and plants.

• **Wildlife:** Animals are preparing for winter. You may observe deer and squirrels feeding, as well as birds traveling south. This is also an excellent time to view animals, as they become more active in preparation for the winter months.

• **Goldenrod and asters,** among other plants, continue to add color and charm to the environment after entering dormancy.

Winter Hiking Precautions

Winter hiking in Missouri may be a peaceful and beautiful experience, but it takes extra planning and caution owing to chilly weather and the possibility of snow or ice.

1. Gear & Clothing.

Proper clothes and equipment are essential for winter hiking.

• **Dress in layers to stay warm and wick away sweat.** Begin with a base layer, then add an insulating layer such as fleece or down, and finally a waterproof, windproof upper layer. Don't forget your thick hat, gloves, and thermal socks.

• **Insulated,** waterproof footwear with strong grip are required. Consider wearing gaiters to prevent snow and ice out of your boots, as well as crampons or microspikes to improve traction on icy routes.

2. Trail conditions.

Winter weather may make paths difficult.

• **Be prepared for snowy and slippery paths.** Use hiking poles for support and balance. Avoid trekking alone in harsh weather, and notify someone of your plans.

• **Navigation:** Snow can obscure route signs and blazes. Use a map, compass, or GPS gadget to remain on track.

3. Safety considerations.

Winter hiking necessitates extra precautions for safety.

• **Monitor for indications of hypothermia** and frostbite. Symptoms of hypothermia include shivering, disorientation, and exhaustion, while frostbite can cause numbness and skin discoloration. Keep warm, dry, and hydrated.

• **Carry emergency supplies** including a first-aid kit, fire starters, and extra food. In the event of an unforeseen delay, a portable emergency shelter or bivvy bag might be quite useful.

4. Wildlife & Flora

Winter alters the environment for plants and animals.

• **Wildlife:** Many animals hibernate or migrate during winter. However, you may still come across deer or traces from other species. Keep an eye out for evidence of animal activity.

• **Evergreen** trees and shrubs offer color to the winter landscape, when other vegetation become dormant. Look for lichens and mosses, which flourish in chilly, wet environments.

Hiking through the seasons in Missouri provides a diverse range of experiences, each with its own distinct charm and challenges. Understanding the special concerns for spring, summer, autumn, and winter will allow you to properly plan your treks and appreciate the state's natural beauty all year. Each season offers its own set of delights, ranging from vivid wildflowers and colorful foliage to peaceful snow-covered vistas. So, embrace the changes of the seasons, dress accordingly, and set out to explore the unique and ever-changing beauty of Missouri's trails.

CHAPTER 13

HIKING WITH PETS

Bringing your pet along on a trek may transform a routine excursion into an unforgettable encounter. Hiking with pets, particularly dogs, may enrich the experience by providing company and an additional layer of enjoyment. As a seasoned hiker who frequently enjoys the trails with my canine companions, I can assure you that, while it takes some more planning and care, the benefits are well worth it. In this chapter, we'll go over everything you need to know about hiking with pets, from planning to safety precautions, to ensure that you and your four-legged companion have a great experience.

Readying Your Pet for a Hike

Before hitting the trail with your pet, make sure they're ready and fit for the experience. Your pet, like you, requires some training and preparation.

1. Assess your pet's fitness level.

• **Prior to hiking,** arrange a vet check-up. Make sure your pet is healthy and up to date on vaccines. If your pet has any chronic diseases or health difficulties, check with your veterinarian to make sure they're ready for hiking.

• **Prepare your pet** for long or arduous excursions by gradually increasing their stamina. Begin with small walks and gradually increase the distance over time. This allows your pet to acclimate to extended durations of physical exercise while lowering the danger of harm.

2. Gear Up

• Invest in a comfortable harness and leash for your pet to use for long amounts of time. A leash is vital for maintaining control, especially on busy paths or in wildlife-rich areas. Consider using a hands-free leash system for extra convenience.

• **Some pets benefit from protective boots,** especially in rugged terrain or harsh weather conditions. Boots keep their paws safe from jagged pebbles, heated pavement, and freezing surfaces.

• Ensure your pet's collar is secure and has an ID tag with current contact information. A microchip is also a smart option for increased security in case your pet goes missing.

3. Training and Commands

• **Teach your pet simple instructions like** "sit," "stay," and "come" before going outside. These instructions may be quite useful for keeping your pet safe and under control on the path.

• **Teach your pet proper trail etiquette,** including keeping on a leash, not pursuing animals, and respecting other hikers. This not only assures safety but also enhances the trekking experience for everyone.

Pet-Friendly Trails

Not all paths are pet-friendly, so pick routes where your pet will feel welcome and secure.

1. Research Trails.

• Check trail rules for pet-friendly policies. Some parks and trails have pet-specific guidelines. Look for paths that clearly accept pets and include facilities such as dog-friendly water and waste disposal stations.

• **Choose trails that are appropriate for your pet's fitness level.** Easy to moderate paths with reasonable terrain are perfect for novices. Avoid routes with harsh conditions or hazards that might harm your pet.

2. Popular Pet-Friendly Trails.

While specific pet-friendly trails differ by location, here are some general suggestions for discovering fantastic options:

• **Local parks and nature reserves provide pet-friendly pathways.** These are often shorter and less strenuous, making them ideal for a leisurely trek with your pet.

• Some national and state parks include pet-friendly hiking trails. Look into certain parks to identify pathways that welcome pets and give facilities for them.

3. Trail features

• **Water sources:** Trails with natural water sources are ideal for dogs to drink and cool down. However, pack extra water and a portable dish to keep your pet hydrated.

• **Look for paths with shady places and rest stops.** These give shade from the sun and a spot for you and your pet to rest.

Safety Advice for Hiking with Pets

Ensuring your pet's safety while hiking is critical for a positive experience. Here are some comprehensive suggestions to keep in mind.

1. Hydration & Nutrition

• **Always pack enough water for yourself and your pet.** Pets are easily dehydrated, especially in warm weather. Bring a foldable bowl so your pet may drink on the move.

• **Pack your pet's normal food and snacks for longer hikes.** This helps individuals stay energized and fulfilled.

2. Health and Comfort

• **Regularly check your pet's paws for wounds,** blisters, and foreign items like thorns. After the trek, clean and examine their paws to avoid infection or injury.

• **Temperature control**: Keep an eye on your pet for any indications of overheating or hypothermia. In hot conditions, watch for symptoms such as heavy panting or drowsiness. In chilly weather, keep your pet warm and dry, and consider using a dog jacket if required.

3. Wildlife & Insects

• **When visiting wildlife areas,** keep your pet on a leash and under supervision. Wild creatures can be unexpected and pose a threat to your pets.

• **Protect your pet against ticks,** fleas, and mosquitoes with proper treatments. Check your pet for ticks after the trek, especially between the toes and around the ears.

4. First Aid

• **Bring a pet-specific first aid kit with bandages,** antiseptic wipes, and tweezers. In the event of an emergency, be familiar with basic first aid for dogs.

• **Prepare a list of area emergency veterinary services** and their contact information. This guarantees that you are prepared in case your pet need medical assistance.

5. Respect for Others

· Maintain trail etiquette by respecting other hikers and trail users. Keep your pet leashed and under control, and clean up after them. This contributes to a great experience for everyone on the route.

• **Be aware of noise levels.** Excessive barking or unruly behavior might disturb other hikers and wildlife. Train your pet to be quiet and courteous on the route.

Hiking with dogs may be quite gratifying, providing company and a shared experience that increases the enjoyment of being outside. By properly planning, selecting the correct routes, and following safety requirements, you can ensure that both you and your pet have a great time on the path. With the proper equipment, training, and planning, you can tackle a broad range of terrain while also enjoying Missouri's natural beauty together. So, pack your pet's kit, schedule a pet-friendly trek, and hit the woods for an excursion you'll both enjoy.

CHAPTER 14

FAMILY HIKING
ADVENTURES

Hiking with your family is an excellent opportunity to bond, make memorable memories, and teach the next generation to the benefits of the great outdoors. As an experienced hiker who has taken my own family on several expeditions, I can guarantee you that with the proper planning, hiking can be a fun experience for everybody, regardless of age. This chapter will go over kid-friendly paths, provide suggestions for hiking with children, and help you choose the best family hiking gear. Let's look at ways to make your family's hiking trips safe, enjoyable, and unforgettable.

Kids-Friendly Trails

Choosing the correct path is critical to providing a great hiking experience for children. Here's what you should look for when choosing kid-friendly trails:

1. Trail Distance and Difficulty

• **For smaller children or beginners,** use shorter routes (preferably no more than 2-3 miles round trip). Shorter treks keep children interested and less likely to become weary or irritated.

• **Select paths with soft**, level terrain. Avoid steep inclines and rough routes that may be difficult for young legs. Flat or moderately undulating pathways are ideal for keeping them interested and energized.

2. Scenic attractions.

• Children are more likely to like trails with fascinating features like waterfalls, scenic overlooks, and animal sightings. Kids like having something to look forward to along the road.

• **Educational opportunities:** Nature centers, interpretive signage, and ranger-led programs are all examples of educational trails that may be both enjoyable and enlightening. This may transform a trek into an educational journey.

3. Safety considerations.

• **Well-marked trails:** Choose routes that are well-marked and simple to follow. Clear signage helps you stay on course and eliminates the possibility of getting lost, which is especially important while hiking with children.

• **Popular routes surrounding parks** with decent facilities, such as bathrooms and water fountains, are ideal for families. Crowded paths may provide a sense of safety and camaraderie while also providing facilities to make the journey simpler.

4. Example of Kid-Friendly Trails

While the precise paths will vary depending on your area, here are some broad ideas to consider:

• **Local parks include short,** simple nature paths with informative signage and interactive displays. These are ideal for young children who may want frequent breaks.

• **Loop trails promote exploration and discovery,** making them more intriguing than out-and-back routes.

Tips for Hiking with Children

Hiking with children takes a little more organization and patience, but it can be quite rewarding. Here are some useful ideas for a smooth and pleasurable hike:

1. Plan ahead and start small. Begin with shorter treks and progressively increase the distance as your children become used to trekking. This improves their stamina and confidence.

• **Involve them in planning.** Allow children to take part in the planning process. Show them maps, talk about the trail's features, and let them choose a few items they want to see along the route. This engagement may increase their excitement.

2. Prepare for comfort.

• Dress your children in layers to adapt to changing weather conditions. Choose moisture-wicking textiles for base layers and pack a waterproof jacket if rain is forecast. Remember to include a hat and gloves for chilly temperatures.

• **Children should wear comfortable,** supportive shoes. Hiking boots or durable shoes with high grip are appropriate. To avoid blisters and pain, avoid wearing brand new shoes.

3. Keep them engaged.

• **Breaks and snacks:** Plan regular stops to relax and snack. Pack a range of snacks that are convenient to consume on the go, such as fruit, almonds, and granola bars. Maintaining high energy levels will help them retain their excitement.

• **Use games and activities** to make the hike more engaging. Scavenger hunts, wildlife bingo, and storytelling are all simple activities that may make the trip more fun and entertaining for children.

4. Safety first.

• Supervise your youngsters, especially near cliffs, streams, or steep areas of the path. Make sure kids grasp basic trail safety regulations, such as sticking on the route and not wandering too far.

• **Carry a basic first aid kit and understand how to use it.** Pack bandages, antiseptic wipes, and pain relievers. Familiarize yourself with basic first aid techniques for common hiking accidents.

5. Be flexible.

• **Adapt to their pace:** Children may need to go slower than adults, which is entirely OK. Allow lots of time to explore and appreciate the surroundings at their leisure.

• **Prepare an exit plan in case your youngster** becomes too weary or agitated during the hike. It's preferable to conclude on a high note and try again another day than to push through and have a poor experience.

Family Hiking Gear

Having the correct gear may significantly improve the comfort and safety of your family trek. Here's a list of important family hiking gear:

1 Backpacks

• **Consider a compact,** lightweight bag for young children to carry their personal stuff, snacks, and water. Make sure it's adaptable and fits comfortably.

• **Parents should have a well-fitted backpack** with enough room for essentials like additional clothing, first aid kits, and food. Look for backpacks with cushioned shoulder straps and a hip belt for enhanced comfort.

2. Hydration & Nutrition

• **Use convenient hydration packs or water bottles.** Make sure each family member has their own water supply and a collapsible dish or cup to share with pets if necessary.

• **Pack a range of snacks to meet everyone's preferences.** Consider portable snacks such as trail mix, dried fruit, cheese sticks, and crackers.

3. Safety Gear

• **Comprehensive First Aid Kit:** Include goods for adults and children. Look for kits that include child-appropriate items and instructions.

• **Sun Protection:** Use high SPF sunscreen, hats, and sunglasses. Children's skin is particularly sensitive, so be cautious while applying and reapplying sunscreen.

4. Clothing: Provide each family member with moisture-wicking base layers, insulating layers for chilly weather, and a waterproof outer layer. Ensure that your attire fits properly and is appropriate for the season.

- **Invest in high-quality hiking boots** or shoes for the entire family. Ensure that they are well-fitted, broken in, and give adequate support and grip.

5. Entertainment and Comfort

- **Comfort items include:** Pack little items to keep children comfortable and occupied, such as a favorite toy, a tiny blanket, or a book for breaks.

- **Emergency gear:** Bring a whistle, a flashlight, and a map of the path. These objects are important in crises and for navigation.

Family hiking trips might be some of the most gratifying experiences you'll have together. With the proper planning, equipment, and attitude, you can plan unforgettable adventures that introduce your children to the delights of nature while also spending quality time together. Choosing kid-friendly routes, planning ahead of time, and prioritizing safety helps ensure that your treks are both pleasant and safe for the entire family. So, pack your gear, assemble your loved ones, and embark on an expedition that will not only allow you to enjoy the great outdoors, but will also improve family relationships and create lasting memories. Happy trekking!

CHAPTER 15

SOLO HIKING TIPS

Going on a solo trek might be one of the most rewarding experiences you can have on the path. There's something truly fulfilling about going out on your own, totally immersed in nature, and being free to travel wherever your soul leads you. Having trekked alone several times, I've grown to love the isolation and self-reliance that solo hiking provides. To guarantee safety and enjoyment, solo hiking must be approached with the appropriate mentality and preparation. This chapter will look at the advantages of hiking alone, highlight important safety warnings, and propose gear designed for solitary explorers.

Advantages of Hiking Alone

Hiking solo has a number of advantages that might improve your outdoor experience. Here's why you should consider hitting the trails on your own:

1. Personal reflection and growth.

• Solo hiking promotes independence and self-reliance. When you're alone on the trail, you're alone accountable for your decisions and actions. This self-sufficiency can boost confidence and problem-solving abilities.

• **Nature offers solitude for contemplation and mental clarity.** You may completely engage with your thoughts and emotions when you are not distracted by the demands of daily life or the desire to collaborate with others.

2. Freedom and Flexibility.

• **Unrestricted route:** Solo hiking allows you to choose your own speed and route. You may pick when to begin, how long to remain at a gorgeous location, and when to return without regard for the preferences or schedules of others.

• **Personal Focus:** You can pursue your passions, such as photography, birding, or simply enjoying the wilderness.

Solo hiking allows you to adapt the experience to what is most important to you.

3. Improved Connection with Nature

• **Explore the Outdoors:** When you're alone, you're more likely to thoroughly absorb your environment. The absence of communication and interruption helps you to connect with nature on a deeper level, from the rustling of leaves to the subtle changes in light.

• **Solo hiking provides greater possibilities** to watch wildlife up close. Animals are more likely to be active and visible when they are not disturbed by a group, providing a more rewarding experience for individuals who like solitude.

Safety precautions for solo hikers

Solo hiking may be extremely gratifying, but it also takes meticulous planning and monitoring to maintain safety. Here are some important measures to consider before and during your solo adventures:

1. Plan and prepare.

• **Select appropriate paths** based on your expertise and fitness level. If this is your first time solo hiking, start with well-marked, popular paths. As your experience grows, you'll be able to explore more isolated and demanding paths.

• **Check trail conditions,** weather predictions, and alerts/closures before heading out. Websites, local ranger stations, and hiking applications can give current information.

2. Inform Others

• **Provide a Trip Plan:** Share your hiking plans with a friend or family member. Provide information about your desired itinerary, approximate start and end timings, and any scheduled pauses. This guarantees that someone knows where you are and may notify authorities if you do not return as scheduled.

• **Maintain an emergency contact** list and keep a charged phone with you at all times. Even if you expect to remain out of cell service area, having a phone is crucial in case of an emergency. If feasible, take a satellite messenger or personal locating beacon in places where there is no service.

3. Stay Aware and Vigilant.

• Trust your instincts. Always believe your gut emotions. If anything doesn't seem right—whether it's the weather, the trail conditions, or even someone you meet—don't be afraid to turn around or change your plans.

• **Stay on marked trails.** To prevent getting lost, stay on recognized paths and use a map or GPS gadget to navigate. Avoid using shortcuts or unmarked pathways, as these might lead to dangerous or confused circumstances.

4. Safety Equipment and Skills.

• **First Aid Knowledge:** Carry a first-aid kit and understand how to use it. Basic first aid skills are required because you will need to handle any injuries or medical difficulties on your own.

• **Consider** self-defense tactics or personal protection supplies, such as pepper spray, when trekking in regions with possible danger from wildlife or humans.

5. Environmental Awareness

• **Prepare for rapid weather changes.** Pack adequate clothing and supplies for the circumstances you anticipate, and be prepared to change your plans if the weather turns bad.

• **Navigation skills:** Learn fundamental navigation skills including reading a map and using a compass. Even if you use a GPS system, you should understand how to navigate without it if required.

Solo Hiking Gear Recommendations

The appropriate gear may significantly improve your comfort and safety while hiking alone. Here's a comprehensive list of kit necessities for solo hiking:

1. Backpack & Storage

• A daypack should be roomy enough to carry basics without becoming too bulky. Choose one with adjustable straps and many sections for orderly storage.

• **Use dry bags to protect** your goods from rain and water crossings. These are especially beneficial for keeping clothing, food, and gadgets dry.

2. Navigation and Communication.

• **Map and compass:** Even if you use a GPS gadget, always have a physical map and compass as a backup. Know how to utilize them to navigate and orient oneself in the event of a device failure.

• **Use a portable GPS device** or smartphone with GPS to navigate unknown or distant paths. Make sure it's completely charged, and consider bringing a portable charger.

• **For distant walks** without phone coverage, a satellite messenger or personal location beacon adds an added layer of safety. These gadgets can broadcast distress signals and interact with emergency responders.

3. Safety and Emergency Equipment:

• **First Aid Kit A small,** well-stocked first aid bag is essential. Include bandages, antibacterial wipes, pain remedies, blister treatment, and any personal prescriptions.

• **Use a whistle to help rescuers locate** you during crises. It's also effective for signaling for assistance in a non-threatening way.

• **Bring a lantern or flashlight** with additional batteries. A headlamp is particularly beneficial since it frees your hands for other chores.

4. Clothing & Shelter

• **Layer your clothing with moisture-wicking base layers,** insulating layers for warmth, and a waterproof upper layer. Layering allows you to modify your apparel in response to changing conditions.

• **For multi-day hikes,** include a lightweight sleeping bag, bivy sack, and small sleeping pad for comfort and insulation.

• **A tiny,** lightweight emergency bivy bag or shelter might give protection if you become trapped or need to stay the night unexpectedly.

5. Food and Hydration.

• **Use a hydration pack** or water bottle with a capacity appropriate for your hike. If you want to get your water from natural streams, bring a water filter or purification tablets.

• **Pack high-energy,** non-perishable foods such as almonds, dried fruit, jerky, and granola bars. These will keep you energized and satisfied during your hike.

Solo hiking is a voyage of self-discovery and adventure, providing unrivaled independence and connection with nature. You may make the most of your solo hiking adventures by recognizing the benefits of hiking alone, taking safety steps, and bringing the correct gear. Embrace the isolation, trust your instincts, and revel in the profound sense of success that comes from navigating the trails alone. Solo hiking allows you to challenge yourself while still enjoying the splendor of the great outdoors. So lace up your boots, grab your kit, and embark on a solo trip that will inspire and motivate you. Happy solo trekking!

CHAPTER 16

GROUP HIKING TIPS

Hiking in a group may turn a simple walk in the woods into an unforgettable journey full of shared experiences and companionship. I've done a lot of group walks, ranging from informal trips with buddies to precisely planned adventures with bigger groups. Each encounter has given me vital lessons about group hiking organization, dynamics management, and safety and etiquette considerations. This chapter will guide you through the complexity of group hiking, allowing everyone to enjoy the adventure while making the most of each other's company.

Planning Group Hikes

A successful group trek requires careful planning. The organizing is essential for ensuring that everyone has a nice time and that the trek goes successfully.

1. Define the purpose and scope.

• **Determine the purpose of the hike.** Are you planning a casual outing, a fitness challenge, or a nature exploration? Understanding the group's goals can help you plan and set expectations.

• **Decide on group size.** Smaller groups of 5–10 individuals are often simpler to manage and keep everyone together. Larger gatherings may need more preparation and organization.

2. Select the Right path

• **Choose a path that matches the group's skills and interests.** Consider the challenge level, length, and terrain. A moderate path with a variety of characteristics is a suitable choice for varied groups.

• **Research the trail extensively.** Investigate trail conditions, possible risks, and any permit or regulatory requirements. Ensure that the path has enough amenities and access points, as needed.

3. Coordinate logistics.

• Determine meeting locations and transportation options. Make sure everyone understands how to get to the trailhead, and consider carpooling to lessen environmental impact and logistical complexity.

• **Set a start and projected** return time. Allow for flexibility while ensuring everyone is aware of the timetable. Include breaks, lunch, and any scheduled stops.

4. Communicate effectively.

• **Use group messaging applications** or email to keep everyone updated. Include vital information such as meeting hours, what to bring, and any specific instructions.

• **Pre-Hike briefing:** Before the trek, advise the group about the plan, including route information, expected conditions, and any rules or guidelines. Ensure that everyone is familiar with the strategy and has the essential equipment.

Managing Group Dynamics

Hiking as a group necessitates balancing individual needs and preferences with shared objectives. Here are some strategies for successfully handling group dynamics:

1. Set expectations.

• **Clarify goals** to ensure everyone knows and agrees on the hike's aims. Whether it's a leisurely stroll or a strenuous workout, setting clear expectations helps to avoid misunderstandings and assures a more enjoyable encounter.

• **Decide** on a tempo that is comfortable for all group members. Be prepared to change the tempo depending on the group's general fitness and preferences.

2. Promote inclusivity.

• **Encourage participation** by including everyone in decision-making and contributing to hiking activities. Allow group members to specify their preferred breaks, routes, and pauses.

• **Be mindful of differences.** Recognize that people's hiking skills and interests vary. Be patient and accommodating, and don't push someone past their comfort level.

3. Handle Challenges

• **Resolve Conflicts:** If a quarrel arises, resolve it calmly and discreetly. Listen to concerns and strive toward a solution that considers everyone's needs and preferences.

• **Optimize group** size by dividing into smaller sub-groups based on pace or interests. This allows for more customized encounters while still keeping the group manageable.

Safety and Group Etiquette

A good group trek relies heavily on safety and correct etiquette. Here's how to keep everyone safe and respectful on the trail:

1. Prioritize safety measures, including first aid and emergency procedures. Have a first aid kit on hand, and make sure at least one person understands basic first aid methods. Create an emergency plan that includes a meeting location in case someone becomes separated.

• **Stay together:** Keep the group together, particularly on unknown or difficult paths. Create a clear mechanism for tracking everyone, such as a designated leader and sweep, to ensure that no one falls behind.

- **Adhere to trail laws and regulations**, including as keeping on indicated trails, respecting animals, and following Leave No Trace principles. This secures the group's safety while also protecting the environment.

2. Practice Trail Etiquette.

- **Be considerate:** Use common politeness on the trail. Yield to speedier walkers or those heading uphill, and be courteous while past others. Maintain a fair noise level to prevent upsetting wildlife or other hikers.

- **Pack out what you pack in.** Leave no trace by packing up all rubbish and debris. Encourage group members to be environmentally conscious and to use best methods for garbage disposal.

- **Share the trail**. If you're hiking in an area with other trail users (e.g., cyclists, equestrians), be mindful of their presence and respect trail etiquette accordingly.

3. Manage group behavior.

- **Promote positive interaction:** Create a cheerful and supportive climate in the group. Encourage everyone to contribute to the group's welfare and morale.

• **Monitor fatigue.** Keep an eye on the group's energy levels and be ready to change plans as required. Take regular pauses to guarantee everyone's comfort and hydration.

• **Prepare for shifting weather conditions.** Bring suitable clothing and supplies for everyone in the group, and be prepared to change plans based on weather forecasts.

Group hiking is a unique and exciting way to experience nature with friends, family, or other explorers. You may create a memorable experience for everyone by carefully planning the trek, managing group dynamics, and following safety and etiquette requirements. Remember that the key to a successful group walk is communication, flexibility, and a common commitment to having fun while preserving the environment. So assemble your company, organize your adventure, and set off on a trek that brings people together while appreciating the beauty of the trails. Happy trekking!

CHAPTER 17

NIGHT HIKING

Night hiking is a completely new type of trip. It provides a one-of-a-kind experience that elevates familiar paths to nearly otherworldly levels. The environment takes on a new dimension under the cover of darkness, and there's something immensely thrilling about exploring the woods when the sun goes down. Having participated in countless night treks, I can assure you that with the proper preparation and mentality, night hiking may be one of the most gratifying and memorable experiences in your hiking repertory. This chapter discusses how to prepare for night treks, as well as safety precautions and necessary equipment for a safe and pleasurable journey.

Planning for Night Hikes

Preparing for a night trip necessitates a shift in perspective and additional considerations over daylight excursions. Here's how to prepare for your midnight expedition.

1. Plan your route.

• **Select a familiar trail:** For your first night trek, stick to a familiar track. Familiarity with the route can alleviate any nervousness about navigating in the dark, allowing you to focus on the experience rather than finding your way.

• **Know the terrain.** Understand the terrain and its possible threats. Even if you're on a known route, dangers like rocks or roots might be difficult to notice at night. Planning allows you to foresee and manage these issues.

• **Check the Moon Phase:** The quantity of natural light available varies depending on the moon phase. A full moon produces greater light, but a new moon causes near-total darkness. Plan your hike based on the moon phase to ensure your comfort level.

2. Inform someone

• **Share your plans:** Inform a friend or family member about your intended route, start time, and projected return time. This guarantees that someone is aware of your whereabouts in case of an emergency.

• **Keep emergency contact information ready,** such as local ranger stations or park services. In the event of an emergency, having a mobile phone or satellite messenger with you might be quite useful.

3. Prepare physically and mentally.

• **Acclimate to low-light circumstances.** This may be accomplished by trekking in twilight or poorly lit situations. It helps your eyes acclimate to darkness and relieves strain.

• **Be mentally prepared.** Night hiking may be unsettling and scary. Mentally prepare for the many sensory stimuli, and trust your equipment and training.

Safety Tips for Night Hiking

When trekking at night, safety is the most important consideration. The darkness brings additional obstacles and threats, therefore suitable preparations are required. Here's how to remain safe on a night hike:

1. Follow the Trail

• **Use marked trails:** Night hiking increases the risk of losing track. To prevent becoming lost, always stick to well defined pathways. Use trail markings and landmarks as a guide to stay on course.

• **Avoid shortcuts and detour from the course.** Unmarked routes can lead to perilous terrain or get you lost, particularly in low-visibility situations.

2. Use proper lighting.

• **Headlamps are essential for night trekking.** It keeps your hands free and delivers steady lighting. Choose a headlight with adjustable brightness and a red light option to protect your night vision.

• **Handheld flashlights** are a useful backup to headlamps. It can be handy for providing more focused light when necessary. Ensure that it has new batteries or is rechargeable.

• **Bring spare batteries** for your headlamp and flashlight. Batteries drain quicker in cold weather, so carrying additional ensures you never go without power.

3. Be aware of your surroundings.

• Listen and observe: Sounds are louder at night. Listen for changes in your surroundings and take note of any movement. Nocturnal creatures are usually more active and might surprise you.

• **Maintain alertness by avoiding distractions** like as phone use and lengthy pauses. Maintain situational awareness by focusing on your surroundings and the terrain.

4. Dress appropriately.

• **Layered clothes:** Temperatures might drop dramatically after dark, so dress in layers. Begin with a moisture-wicking base layer, then add insulating layers before finishing with a windproof or waterproof outer layer.

• **Wear sturdy,** comfortable hiking footwear with adequate traction. The dark makes it difficult to see the route, so strong boots will help you cross rough terrain securely.

Gear and Lighting

The appropriate equipment may make or ruin a night trek. Here's a thorough look at the necessary equipment and lights for a successful and safe nocturnal adventure:

1. Headlamps:

• **Select a headlight** with adjustable brightness and beam distance for optimal hiking experience. A headlight with at least 100 lumens is usually enough for most night walks.

• **Comfort and fit:** Ensure that the headlamp is comfortable to wear and has an adjustable strap. It should fit comfortably on your head, especially when worn for a lengthy period of time.

• **Red light mode improves** night vision and reduces glare. It's particularly beneficial for navigating and interpreting maps.

2. flashlights

• **Choose a flashlight that is durable and weatherproof.** It should be able to survive falls and exposure to the weather, which are typical on night walks.

• **Look for flashlights with adjustable beam settings.** A concentrated beam is excellent for locating distant things, but a wide beam illuminates a larger area around you.

• **Rechargeable flashlights are environmentally beneficial** and cost-effective in the long term. Before you go, be sure you have a stable power source to recharge.

3. Spare Batteries

• **Carry extra batteries for your headlamp and flashlight.** Pack spares that are compatible with the batteries used by your devices.

• **Store extra batteries in** a weatherproof container to avoid moisture and freezing temperatures. Cold temperatures might affect battery performance, so keep them near your body for warmth.

4. Navigation Tools

• **Map and Compass:** Even with lights, it's possible to become disoriented at nighttime. Carry a map and compass, and understand how to use them. They provide a solid backup in the event that electrical gadgets fail.

• **A GPS gadget** is useful for night trekking, especially on unfamiliar paths. Make sure it is completely charged, and bring a portable charger if required.

5. Emergency Gear

• **A lightweight emergency blanket** or bivy sack can give warmth and protection if you become stuck or need to spend the night unexpectedly.

• **Use a whistle to signal** for aid, as it may be heard from a considerable distance. It's a modest yet important item to carry.

• **A multi-tool with capabilities** like a knife, pliers, and screwdrivers can help cope with unanticipated situations on the trail.

Night hiking provides a variety of unique sensations and difficulties. The darkness transforms the familiar into the intriguing, providing a new perspective on the paths you enjoy. You may make the most of your night treks by properly preparing, emphasizing safety, and equipping yourself with the appropriate equipment.

Remember that night hiking is more than just navigating in the dark; it's also about enjoying the particular beauty and calm that evening lends to the route. So, pack your stuff, plot your route, and face the night with courage and curiosity. The trails are waiting, and the journey has just begun. Happy trekking tonight!

CHAPTER 18

HIKING DURING COVID-19

Hiking has always been my sanctuary—a place where I can find calm, clarity, and a connection to nature. However, the COVID-19 epidemic posed an unexpected challenge to this popular hobby. Hiking during the pandemic has necessitated a new approach due to limits, guidelines, and a greater understanding of our influence on both the environment and one another. This chapter will teach you how to be safe, navigate trails properly, and embrace methods that respect both public health and the great outdoors.

Safety Guidelines

The epidemic changed the way we engage with our surroundings and other hikers. Implementing good safety precautions is critical for safeguarding ourselves and others while also enjoying the trails.

1. Follow local regulations.

• **Stay informed:** Regulations and standards may differ by locale and even each route. Before you leave, check local health department warnings, park websites, or trail management authority for the most recent information on closures, capacity limitations, and special rules.

• **Respect restrictions:** Follow any limits on trail access, parking, or group sizes. These steps are intended to reduce overcrowding and the danger of viral transmission.

2. Social distancing

• **Maintain distance.** Keep a safe distance from other hikers, preferably at least 6 feet. This approach reduces the potential of viral transmission, particularly in congested places or small portions of the route.

• **Select off-peak times:** If possible, trek when the paths are less congested. Early mornings and weekdays are frequently calmer and allow for greater social separation.

3. Mask Wearing and Hygiene.

• **Wear a mask in locations** where social separation is not possible, such parking lots, trailheads, or limited trails. Masks assist to restrict the spread of droplets, protecting both you and others.

• **Use hand sanitizer** containing at least 60% alcohol often, especially after handling public surfaces like trailhead kiosks or picnic tables.

• **Avoid touching your face.** Avoid touching your face to lessen the danger of germs spreading from your hands to your mouth, nose, or eyes.

4. Health precautions.

• **Check Your Health:** Before leaving, make sure you're healthy and free of COVID-19 symptoms. If you're sick or have been exposed to someone who has the virus, remain at home to avoid spreading it.

- **Be vigilant of COVID-19 symptoms,** including fever, cough, and trouble breathing. Monitor your health and get medical attention if necessary.

Safe Navigation of Trails

Hiking during the pandemic necessitates extra caution to ensure you navigate trails safely while keeping to health requirements.

1. Plan ahead of time.

- **Choose less crowded pathways.** This helps you avoid large gatherings and maintain social separation.

- **Verify trail conditions** and identify potential dangers caused by recent weather or increased traffic. Trail applications or websites can provide real-time updates.

2. Be Prepared:

- **Pack essentials.** Bring all required supplies, such as a mask, hand sanitizer, and extra water. Do not rely on public facilities or amenities, since they may be closed or unavailable.

• **Pack out all rubbish and waste.** Leave No Trace ethics are more crucial than ever, as waste and litter can pose health problems in today's environment.

3. Navigation and Safety

• **Follow marked trails.** Stick to defined routes to avoid getting lost and to reduce your influence on natural areas. Deviating from specified pathways can result in accidents and greater environmental impact.

• **Prepare an emergency** plan and identify the nearest hospital or medical institution. Carry a fully charged mobile phone in case of an emergency, and make sure you know how to reach local emergency services.

4. Respect others.

• **Allow other hikers** to pass while maintaining a safe distance. This politeness helps to avoid near interactions and keep everyone safe.

• **Keep hiking** groups small and minimize chatting on the path. Larger crowds can heighten the danger of viral transmission and limit the trail's capacity.

Safe Hiking Practices

Adopting appropriate hiking behaviors is critical not just for your own safety, but also for the well-being of other hikers and the environment.

1. Respect trail etiquette and follow local guidelines. Follow any extra local guidelines or requests from trail management. They may have established particular guidelines for managing trail usage during the outbreak.

· **Demonstrate courtesy** and tolerance with other hikers. Everyone is navigating this new reality together, and maintaining a cheerful attitude makes the process more pleasurable for everyone.

2. Minimize Impact:

• Stick to designated pathways and avoid building new shortcuts. Staying on established routes helps to maintain plants and decreases erosion, so protecting the pathway for future hikers.

• **Follow Leave No Trace guidelines strictly.** Pack out all rubbish, including food scraps and personal things, to reduce your environmental effect.

3. Support local trails.

• **Donate and volunteer:** Consider contributing or volunteering for groups that preserve and protect trails. Supporting these groups ensures that trails are accessible and well-maintained.

• **Encourage responsible hiking:** Share your expertise and urge others to use safe and responsible hiking techniques. The more people who are aware, the better the hiking experience for everybody.

4. Adapt and be flexible.

• **Be prepared to adapt:** Prepare for abrupt changes in regulations or situations. Flexibility and adaptation are essential, as standards and trail conditions may alter in response to the expanding epidemic.

• Prepare a backup plan in case of crowded trailheads or unexpected closures. Exploring lesser-known paths or exploring different outdoor regions may be a safe and entertaining activity.

Hiking during COVID-19 presented new difficulties and obligations. While the epidemic has changed our approach to outdoor activities, it has also underlined the necessity of safety, respect, and awareness. We may appreciate nature's beauty while protecting ourselves and others by adhering to safety requirements, traversing paths carefully, and practicing responsible hiking.

The paths are still there, ready to be discovered, and the natural environment remains a source of comfort and regeneration. As we navigate this new era of hiking, let us do it with caution and responsibility. Embrace the experience, follow the rules, and enjoy the peace and quiet that nature provides, all while keeping the community and the environment in mind. Happy trekking, and be cautious out there!

CHAPTER 19

ADVANCED HIKING
TECHNIQUES

For those of us who have been hiking for years and want to take our abilities to the next level, learning advanced hiking methods is an exciting and satisfying task. This chapter discusses climbing and scrambling, traversing rivers and rough terrain, and long-distance hiking techniques. These sophisticated approaches need a combination of expertise, planning, and a fair dose of adventurous spirit. So lace up your boots, pack your stuff, and let's get into the more technical parts of hiking.

Climbing and scrambling

Climbing and scrambling transform hiking from a relaxing day to a full-fledged activity. These approaches require crossing high or near-vertical rock cliffs and rough terrain, which can put your physical and mental capabilities to the test. Here's a thorough look at how to approach these difficult areas safely and successfully.

1. Understanding climbing and scrambling

• **Climbing entails** using ropes, harnesses, and climbing gear to ascend steep inclines or vertical rock cliffs. Climbing necessitates technical expertise and the ability to utilize equipment correctly.

• **Scrambling:** While less complex than climbing, scrambling includes utilizing hands and feet to navigate steep or rocky terrain. It sits midway between hiking and climbing and is often done on less steep terrain.

2. Gear & Equipment

• **Required climbin**g gear includes harnesses, shoes, ropes, carabiners, nuts, and cams. Each piece of gear has a unique purpose in guaranteeing your safety when scaling rock faces.

- **Scrambling Gear:** Hiking boots with strong grip are essential for scrambling, although it does not require as much equipment as climbing. For more difficult scrambles, gloves and a helmet may be beneficial.

3. Technique & Safety

- **Climbing techniques:** Focus on methods such as good foot placement, keeping three points of contact (two hands and one foot, or two feet and one hand), and using your legs for strength rather than your arms alone.

- **Scrambling techniques:** When scrambling, search for natural handholds and footholds. Use your body weight to your advantage while maintaining a low center of gravity. Balance is essential, so move carefully and test each grip before placing your entire weight on it.

- **Safety measures:** Always wear a safety harness and helmet when climbing. Before you begin your ascent, double-check all knots and gear. When scrambling, consider the rock condition and avoid loose or unstable portions.

Crossing the Water and Rocky Terrain

Crossing water and crossing difficult terrain require both skill and prudence. These portions of a hike can be challenging, but with the appropriate technique, they can be completed safely.

1. Assess the Water Crossing: Before attempting to cross a stream or river, consider the depth, current speed, and any dangers, such as slippery rocks. Look for safer crossing options, such as shallow regions or locations with solid crossing logs.

• **Crossing techniques:** Use trekking poles to keep yourself stable as you cross. Position them in front of you to determine the depth and stability of the streambed. Cross at an angle, facing upstream, to decrease the current's influence on your balance.

• **Safety Tip:** If the water is quick or deep, consider taking a different path or waiting for better circumstances. Never attempt to cross if the water level is higher than your knees if you are unsure of the current's strength.

2. Navigating rocky terrain

• **Foot placement:** To avoid sliding or twisting your ankle on rough ground, set your feet properly. Step on flat areas and utilize rocks with a solid foundation. Before putting your whole weight on rocks, test their stability.

• **Use trekking poles:** Trekking poles can improve stability on difficult terrain. Use them to assess rock stability and maintain balance.

• **Avoiding hazards:** Keep an eye out for loose rocks and scree that may move underfoot. Maintain a steady speed and avoid hurrying, as this increases the likelihood of an accident. Use a spotter whenever necessary, especially while traversing difficult areas.

3. Long-Distance Hiking Strategies.

lengthy-distance hiking, whether a multi-day journey or a part of a lengthy path, necessitates meticulous preparation and strategy. Here's how to plan and manage long-distance hikes:

• **Training and Conditioning:** Increase endurance with lengthy treks, weight training, and aerobic activity. Gradually increase the duration and complexity of your hikes to get your body ready for prolonged effort.

• **Planning and resupply:** Plan your itinerary and mark replenishment sites for food and water. Make sure you have a comprehensive map and an understanding of the area. Pack lightly, but include enough basic items to get you through the journey.

• Create a pacing and rest strategy to ensure consistent growth without overexertion. Take regular pauses and be hydrated and well-nourished.

• Use GPS and maps to track progress and keep on course. Be careful of trail signs and landmarks to ensure you're on the right track.

• **Dealing with Fatigue:** Listen to your body and alter your speed accordingly. Ensure you receive enough sleep and rest every night, especially on multi-day hikes.

Advanced hiking skills provide a new level of adventure and difficulty. Whether you're ascending a rock face, crossing a stream, or starting on a long-distance expedition, mastering these abilities necessitates planning, practice, and a strong respect for the area.

Accept the task with confidence and eagerness to learn. Each climb, scramble, and river crossing provide a chance to broaden your abilities and strengthen your relationship to the environment. With the correct equipment, tactics, and mentality, you may not only overcome these advanced hiking problems, but also improve your whole hiking experience.

So get out there, challenge yourself, and let the trails teach you new things. Adventure beckons, and the mountains call. Happy trekking, and may your adventures be safe and exciting!

CHAPTER 20

MAINTAINING YOUR GEAR

After numerous trips through deep forests, harsh slopes, and meandering paths, I've discovered that keeping my hiking gear in good condition is critical for both safety and performance. Proper maintenance not only increases the life of your equipment, but also guarantees that you're prepared for whatever adventure comes your way. In this chapter, we'll get into the details of cleaning and repairing equipment, correctly storing gear, and determining whether to update or replace it. Whether you're a seasoned trekker or a weekend warrior, these recommendations will help you keep your gear in top condition.

Cleaning and Repairing Equipment

Regular cleaning and maintenance are the first steps in keeping your gear in good working order. Dirt, dampness, and wear may all degrade your equipment, so it's critical to keep up with maintenance.

1. Cleaning Techniques.

• **Shake backpacks after hikes,** especially muddy ones, to remove loose dirt and debris. Refer to the manufacturer's instructions for a more thorough cleaning. Most backpacks may be hand-washed using mild soap and water. Scrub difficult places with a gentle brush or cloth. Avoid machine washing if it is not suggested since it might harm the fabric and cause additional wear. To avoid mold and mildew, completely dry your backpack before storing it.

• **Trekking poles:** After each hike, wipe the trekking poles down with a moist towel. Pay careful attention to the grips, since they can collect perspiration and grime. If your poles have removable baskets, clean them individually. For a more thorough cleaning, remove the poles and wash the pieces with mild soap and water. To prevent rust, ensure they are thoroughly dry before reassembling.

Why Proper footwear upkeep is essential for comfort and safety. Brush your footwear after each trek to remove any loose dirt or mud. To clean the outside more thoroughly, scrub it with a mixture of water and mild soap. Avoid wetting the boots since too much moisture might ruin the leather or fabric. Waterproof boots should be treated according to the manufacturer's recommendations. To keep your boots in good condition, always allow them to dry naturally away from direct heat.

• **Sleeping bags and pads:** Follow the care directions on the label. Spot-clean stains on sleeping bags when they occur and launder them on occasion. Fill a front-loading washer or a big sink with cold water and light detergent. Avoid using fabric softener. Dry your sleeping bag properly in a big drier or let it air dry flat. Sleeping pads should be cleaned out with a moist cloth and mild soap, not submerged. Make sure they are completely dry before storing.

2. Repairing Gear

• **For tiny tears or holes in backpacks,** use a patch kit specialized for outdoor gear. Clean the area surrounding the rip, apply the patch as directed, and allow it heal fully before using the backpack again. Consider hiring an expert to fix more substantial damage.

• **Trekking poles:** If your trekking poles have difficulties like blocked sections or broken tips, check the manufacturer's warranty and repair alternatives. Many hiking pole brands provide replacement parts and repair services.

• **Repair small tears** or holes in boots using specialist shoe repair kits. For more serious damage, take your boots to a professional cobbler, who can repair broken eyelets and cracked soles.

• **To repair tiny** tears in sleeping bags or pads, use repair patches or specialist adhesive. Make sure the region is clean and dry before putting the patch. For more substantial repairs, expert assistance may be required.

Proper Storage of Gear

Proper storage is vital for extending the life of your gear and ensuring that it is ready for your next excursion. Here are some suggestions for keeping various sorts of hiking equipment:

1 Backpacks

• **Keep your backpack clean and dry.** Moisture may cause mildew and foul smells. To keep the form of the compartments and prevent strain on the zippers, make sure they are all empty and unzipped.

• **Store your bag in a cool,** dry area away from direct sunlight to prevent fading and fabric degradation.

• Stuff your backpack with paper or cloth to keep it in shape. This also keeps the cloth from becoming deformed or wrinkled over time.

2. Storing Trekking Poles

• **Keep poles dry and tidy.** Collapsible poles should be fully retracted and stored in a dry place to avoid rusting.

• Use a storage container or a designated area in your gear closet to prevent damage. Avoid resting them against walls or other things where they might be twisted or damaged.

3. Footwear

• **Keep footwear clean and dry.** Remove the insoles and allow them to air out separately to avoid smells and mold.

Stuff the boots with newspaper or boot shapers to keep them in shape.

• Store boots away from direct heat sources, such as radiators or sunny locations, to prevent drying and cracking.

4. Sleeping bags and pads.

• **Keep sleeping bags and pads entirely dry.** To avoid compressing the insulation, store sleeping bags in a big storage sack or hang them in a cool, dry spot.

• To maintain insulating efficiency, avoid storing sleeping bags and pads in stuff sacks for lengthy durations.

Upgrading and Replacing Gear:

Even with proper maintenance, gear will eventually need to be replaced or updated. Knowing when and how to change your equipment will help you have a better hiking experience and stay safe.

1. Evaluating Gear Condition

• Visual Inspection Inspect your gear on a regular basis for signs of wear and tear. Look for frayed straps, worn-out soles, or rusty parts. If you observe substantial damage or reduced performance, it may be time to update.

• **If your gear is no longer performing as intended,** such as a sleeping bag or boots, consider replacing it. Poorly performing gear might have an influence on your trail safety and comfort.

2. Upgrading Gear:

• **Evaluate needs.** Consider upgrading if your existing gear isn't meeting your demands or if you want to take on more difficult excursions. For example, if you're progressing from day walks to multi-day treks, you may want more advanced equipment, such as a high-quality tent or a more robust backpack.

• **Before upgrading,** investigate the latest gear alternatives and reviews. Look for gear that improves performance, uses better materials, or has additional features that are appropriate for your hiking style and needs.

• **Try before you buy.** Whenever feasible, try out or rent gear before making a purchase. This ensures that it fits properly and matches your expectations.

3. Replacing Gear:

• **Replace worn-out or unsafe gear.** This includes things like worn-out footwear, damaged bags, and faulty safety gear.

• **Monitor improvements in gear technology.** Newer versions frequently have superior performance, lighter materials, and other features to enhance your hiking experience.

• Prioritize gear replacement depending on safety and comfort considerations. Set a budget. Investing in high-quality gear might save you money in the long term.

Maintaining your hiking equipment is more than simply maintaining it in excellent condition; it's also about assuring your safety, comfort, and enjoyment on the trails. You'll be ready for any adventure if you keep your gear clean and repaired on a regular basis, store it appropriately, and know when to update or replace it.

Remember that your gear is an investment in your outdoor adventures. Treat it well, and it will be your devoted companion on innumerable walks and excursions. With the right care and attention, you'll be ready to explore new paths and make unforgettable experiences in the great outdoors

CHAPTER 21

HIKING FOR FITNESS AND WELLNESS

As an experienced hiker, I've grown to recognize that hiking is more than simply exploring new routes or finding magnificent views; it's also an excellent approach to improve overall health and wellness. Over time, I've seen directly how hiking has enhanced my physical health, mental clarity, and general feeling of well-being. In this chapter, we'll look at the numerous health advantages of hiking, how to design a hiking fitness plan based on your objectives, and how to integrate hiking with other activities for a total wellness approach.

Health Benefits of Hiking

Hiking has several health advantages, making it an excellent choice for both physical and emotional well-being. Let me go over some of the primary perks I've discovered on the trails.

1. Cardiovascular Health.

Hiking is an excellent cardiovascular workout. As you traverse different terrains, your heart works harder to circulate blood and oxygen throughout your body. This persistent exertion boosts cardiovascular endurance, decreases blood pressure, and regulates cholesterol levels. On a steep climb or a hard course, your heart rate will rise, giving a natural and practical approach to improve your heart health.

2. Muscle strength and tone.

Walking on uneven terrain and climbing hills use a variety of muscle groups. Hiking works the muscles in your legs, core, and upper body, especially if you use trekking poles. Climbing uphill or navigating uneven routes helps you improve endurance and tone muscles that may not receive as much attention in other types of training.

3. Joint Health.

Hiking is less strenuous on your joints than high-impact exercises like jogging. Trail surfaces give natural cushioning, which helps to lessen stress on your knees and hips. Furthermore, the diverse terrain and gradual inclines provide a low-impact method for maintaining joint flexibility and mobility.

4. Weight Management.

Hiking is a great method to burn calories and control your weight. Depending on the intensity and duration of your journey, you can burn between 400 and 700 calories each hour. Hiking is an excellent strategy to maintain a healthy weight or lose a few pounds since it combines aerobic workout with muscular involvement.

5. Mental Health and Stress Reduction.

One of the most enjoyable parts of hiking is the positive influence it has on mental health. Spending time in nature relieves stress, anxiety, and boosts mood. The peacefulness of the natural surroundings, along with physical exertion, promotes the release of endorphins, your body's natural mood enhancers. For me, the silence of the forest or the panoramic vistas from a summit always bring a sense of calm and mental clarity.

6. Improved Sleep Regular physical exercise, like hiking, can lead to better sleep habits. Physical activity and exposure to natural light help regulate your sleep-wake cycle, resulting in a more peaceful sleep. After a day on the trails, I frequently sleep better and wake up feeling invigorated.

Creating a Hiking Fitness strategy

To include hiking into your fitness regimen or utilize it as a major form of exercise, an organized strategy can help you reach your objectives. Here's my method to creating a hiking fitness plan:

1. Determine your current fitness level.

Before beginning any new fitness program, it is critical to analyze your existing fitness level. Assess your cardiovascular endurance, strength, and flexibility. This will allow you to identify the intensity and duration of treks that are appropriate for you, as well as measure your development over time.

2. Set clear goals.

Determine what you hope to achieve with your hiking activity. Are you want to enhance your cardiovascular health, gain muscle, or reduce weight? Setting clear, quantifiable objectives will help you organize your training routine. For example, you may set a goal of hiking for 30 minutes three times each week, gradually increasing the duration and intensity as your endurance improves.

3. Plan your hiking schedule.

Consistency is essential in any workout strategy. Make hiking a part of your weekly routine by scheduling it on specified days and times. If you're just starting out, start with shorter, simpler treks and gradually increase the length and difficulty as your stamina improves. Make careful to schedule rest days to enable your body to heal and avoid overuse issues.

4. Incorporate interval training.

To get the most out of hiking, try including interval training into your regimen. Alternate between high-intensity hiking (e.g., ascending steep inclines) and moderate-intensity strolling on level terrain. This method improves cardiovascular fitness and endurance while keeping your workouts diverse and interesting.

5. Track your progress.

Keep a hiking notebook or use a fitness app to log your hikes, measure your progress, and remain inspired. Note the distance, elevation gain, length, and how you felt during and after each trek. Tracking your progress keeps you on track toward your goals and allows you to enjoy your accomplishments along the way.

6. Add Strength and Flexibility Training

Hiking is great for cardiovascular health and muscular conditioning, but adding strength and flexibility workouts will help you improve your overall fitness. Complement your trekking practice with exercises such as weight training, yoga, or Pilates. Stronger core and leg muscles will enhance your hiking performance while lowering your chance of injury.

7. Stay hydrated and eat well.

Proper diet and water are essential for staying energized and improving your hiking performance. Consume a balanced diet high in whole foods, lean proteins, and healthy fats. Stay hydrated by drinking lots of water prior to, during, and after your hikes. Proper fuelling and hydration promote physical activity and improve recovery.

Combining Hiking and Other Activities

Combining hiking with other activities might help you achieve a well-rounded fitness program. This strategy helps to avoid boredom, improves overall fitness, and guarantees that you engage diverse muscle areas. Here are several methods to combine hiking with other types of exercise:

1. Cross-training.

Incorporate cross-training exercises into your workout program to boost your general strength, flexibility, and cardiovascular endurance. Cycling, swimming, and rowing give good cardiovascular benefits while also strengthening muscles that may not be completely engaged when trekking. Cross-training also lowers the chance of overuse injuries by changing up your workout routine.

2. Strength Training Including strength training in your hiking program can improve performance and avoid injuries. Squats, lunges, step-ups, and core exercises are good options for targeting the muscles utilized during hiking. Strength training helps to develop the muscle strength and endurance required for tough courses.

3. Flexibility and Mobility.

Incorporate flexibility and mobility exercises into your daily routine to increase your range of motion and prevent stiffness. Yoga, stretching, and foam rolling can help you retain flexibility and minimize muscular tightness. These routines enhance hiking by increasing overall mobility quality and lowering the chance of injury.

4. Outdoor Activities.

If you enjoy being outside, consider incorporating more outdoor activities into your schedule. Trail jogging, mountain biking, and kayaking are all great ways to go outside and stay active. Combining multiple outdoor activities keeps your routine interesting and allows you to explore other settings.

5. Rest and Recovery.

Don't underestimate the value of rest and recuperation in your workout regimen. Allow your body to rest in between exercises and treks to avoid overtraining and injury. Rest days, appropriate sleep, and activities such as moderate stretching or meditation can all help with recuperation.

Hiking is more than simply a recreational activity; it's an effective way to improve physical fitness and general well-being. You may optimize the benefits of hiking by learning about the multiple health benefits, developing a planned fitness plan, and incorporating hiking into other activities. Whether you're hiking for cardiovascular health, muscle strength, or stress release, incorporating hiking into your workout program may result in major physical and mental health benefits.

So, lace up your hiking boots, hit the trails, and begin experiencing the benefits of this energizing sport. Accept the adventure, be persistent, and reap the numerous benefits that hiking provides in your life. Here's to your health and wellness—and happy trekking!

CHAPTER 22

RESOURCES AND
ADDITIONAL
INFORMATION

When it comes to hiking, having the correct resources may make a huge difference. Over the years, I've discovered that connecting with local groups, participating in online forums, and keeping an eye out for forthcoming events may dramatically improve your hiking experience. In this chapter,

I'll walk you through some useful tools and supplementary information to keep you informed, motivated, and inspired on your hiking trips.

Local Hiking Organizations

Local hiking groups are excellent tools for anybody wishing to strengthen their connection to the hiking community, participate in conservation initiatives, or just learn about the finest trails and hiking activities in their region. Here's an overview of several main sorts of organizations and how they may help you:

1. Regional Hiking Clubs

Joining a regional hiking club may be a great way to become involved in the hiking community. These clubs frequently plan group treks, workshops, and social gatherings. For example, groups such as the Missouri Trail Association and the Ozark Trail Association give a lot of information about local trails and also provide volunteer opportunities for trail maintenance. Joining such a group not only allows you to explore new paths, but it also links you with others who share your enthusiasm for hiking.

2. Conservation Groups

Conservation groups play an important role in conserving hiking routes and natural habitats. The Nature Conservancy and Missouri Botanical Garden's Natural Areas Program work diligently to conserve and preserve natural ecosystems. By sponsoring or helping with these groups, you help to preserve the landscapes you like exploring. Many of these organizations host activities such as trail cleanups, tree plantings, and educational presentations.

3. Park and Recreation Departments

Local and state park administrations frequently provide hikers with maps, route information, and safety instructions. Departments like Missouri State Parks and City Parks and Recreation give up-to-date information on trail conditions, upcoming activities, and permits. They also provide educational seminars and guided treks to improve your outdoor experience.

4. Outdoor Gear Shops

While not technically an organization, local outdoor gear stores are great resources. They frequently contain bulletin boards with details on local hiking activities, trail conditions, and gear advice. Furthermore, the workers at these businesses are typically experienced hikers who can provide individual advise and recommendations.

Online Community and Forums

The internet era has made it simpler than ever to communicate with other hikers and learn about trails, gear, and hiking suggestions. Online communities and forums may be valuable tools for seeking advice, exchanging experiences, and staying up to speed on hiking news. Here's a look at some of the best internet resources:

1. Hiking Forums

Online forums, such as Back packer. com's Forums or Trail space Forums, allow hikers to debate trails, gear, and skills. Threads may be found on practically any hiking-related topic, including the finest local trails, gear evaluations, and hiking safety guidelines. Participating in these forums allows you to ask questions, share your own experiences, and learn from other hikers.

2. Social Media Groups

There are several hiking-related groups and pages on social media platforms such as Facebook and Instagram. Joining organizations like Hiking Missouri or following hashtags like #MissouriHiking will keep you updated on local treks, meetups, and trail conditions. These organizations frequently exchange images, trip reports, and tips, which may be quite useful when planning your own treks.

3. Hiking Apps

Hiking applications like AllTrails, Gaia GPS, and Hiking Project provide trail maps, reviews, and GPS tracking. These applications are ideal for exploring new routes, reading about other hikers' experiences, and navigating while on the go. Many of these applications also have community elements, allowing you to connect with other hikers and participate in group treks or challenges.

4. Youtube Channels and Blogs

There are countless YouTube channels and websites dedicated to hiking and outdoor activities. Channels like The Hiking Project and websites like Section Hiker provide gear evaluations, trail guides, and hiking advice. Watching movies and reading blog entries may give visual and comprehensive information on trails and gear that may be valuable for your own travels.

Upcoming Events and Hikes

Keeping track of forthcoming events and treks might provide a new depth to your hiking habit. There are several possibilities to become involved, including joining a group hike, participating in a trail running event, and attending a hiking class. Here's how to remain up to date:

1. Event calendars

Many hiking groups, park agencies, and outdoor organizations include event calendars on their websites. Missouri State Parks, for example, frequently posts announcements about forthcoming activities such as guided hikes, educational programs, and volunteer opportunities. Regularly checking these calendars might help you identify events that are relevant to your interests and schedule.

2. Local Hiking Meetups

Hiking and outdoor activities are frequently discussed in groups on websites such as Meetup.com. Joining these clubs allows you to connect with local hikers and learn about scheduled treks and activities. Whether it's a casual weekend hike or a more scheduled event, meetings are an excellent opportunity to discover new routes and meet new friends.

3. Trail Running and Adventure Races

For those who want a little extra challenge, trail running events and adventure races can be a great addition to your hiking routine. Events such as the Ozark Trail 100 and the Missouri Trail Series provide possibilities for competitive hiking and trail running. These races are frequently advertised on race-specific websites or by local running groups.

4. Workshops and Clinics

Attending courses and clinics might help you improve your hiking abilities and knowledge. Look for events sponsored by local outdoor businesses or hiking clubs that cover topics such as navigation, first aid, and wilderness survival. These educational opportunities are both beneficial and enjoyable.

Navigating the world of hiking may be really gratifying, especially when you have the necessary resources and information at your disposal. Connecting with local hiking groups, participating in online communities, and getting up to speed on forthcoming events may help you expand your hiking experience while also building a supporting network of fellow hikers.

These tools are designed to help you volunteer, discover new trails, or simply connect with people who share your love. So be active, remain informed, and, most importantly, keep exploring and enjoying the amazing world of hiking. Here's to many adventures and pleasant trails!

CHAPTER 23

APPENDIX

When it comes to hiking, preparation is essential for a safe and fun trip. This appendix is a valuable guide to assist you manage any obstacles you may face on the trail. From emergency contacts to handy apps, these sections are intended to offer you with essential information and tools. Let's get into each section in depth.

Emergency Contacts

A list of emergency contacts might come in handy if something goes wrong while hiking. It's critical to know who to call and how to receive assistance fast.

1. Local Emergency Services

Always save the phone number for local emergency services. In the United States, this is usually 911. However, in certain distant regions, you may need to call special municipal or park emergency numbers.

For example:

• For emergencies, contact the National Park Service at 1-877-696-6775.

• Find the State Park Rangers phone number for the park you're visiting (usually available on park websites or visitor centers).

2. Local Search and Rescue Teams

Search and rescue teams specialize in discovering and aiding hikers in difficulty. Contact information for these groups is often accessible via local park services or trail associations. Some states or areas also have specific SAR teams, such as the Missouri Search and Rescue teams, which you may contact if you become lost or want quick assistance.

3. Park or Trail Information Centers

Many major hiking destinations feature information centers or ranger stations that can assist in emergencies. It's vital to have the contact information for these facilities since they can provide immediate aid or coordinate with rescue crews.

4. Personal Emergency Contact List

Always tell someone about your trekking plans, including your planned return time. This might be a friend, relative, or neighbor. If something goes wrong and you don't return as scheduled, they can notify the authorities. Provide details such as:

• Your destination.

• The track you're taking.

• Expected return time.

Maps and Navigation Tools

To efficiently navigate the trails, you'll need the correct maps and tools. Here's an in-depth look at the alternatives available:

1. Physical Maps

Physical maps are quite useful for trekking. They offer a clear perspective of the routes, scenery, and landmarks. Topographic maps are very valuable since they depict elevation variations and specific topographical characteristics. Physical maps are available at outdoor gear stores, park visitor centers, and online from sources such as the US Geological Survey (USGS).

Tips:

• Always have a paper map as a backup for technological gadgets.

• Familiarize yourself with map symbols and scales before leaving.

2. GPS devices

Handheld GPS systems provide reliable position tracking, which is especially useful in unfamiliar environments. Devices like Garmin or Magellan can give real-time position, altitude, and distance information. If you're planning a lengthy hike, make sure your smartphone is fully charged and consider packing extra batteries.

Tips:

• Download maps and waypoints before leaving to avoid losing signal.

• Check your device's battery regularly and have a backup power source in case of necessity.

3. Smartphone Apps

Smartphone apps such as AllTrails, Gaia GPS, and Komoot provide extensive trail maps, navigation tools, and tracking capabilities. These applications may be quite useful for planning treks and navigating. They frequently contain user evaluations and trail conditions, which may be really useful.

Tips:

• Ensure your phone is fully charged and have a portable charger.

• Download offline maps to reduce reliance on mobile service.

4. Compass

A compass is an essential tool for navigating. While it may appear outdated in the age of GPS, it remains a dependable method of orienting yourself if technological gadgets fail. Learning how to use a compass with a map is an essential skill for any hiker.

Tips:

• Try out your compass before setting out to verify you're familiar with it.

• Carry a compass, even if you mostly use GPS.

Additional Reading and References

Increasing your understanding of hiking, trails, and outdoor safety is always useful. Here are some suggested resources for further reading.

1. Hiking Guides

Books and guides include detailed information about routes, local flora and animals, and hiking skills. Some recommended titles are:

• Johnny Molloy's "Hiking Missouri" provides a detailed reference of trails throughout Missouri.

- "The Ultimate Hiker's Gear Guide" by Andrew Skurka provides tips on gear and planning.

2. Safety and Survival Manuals

Understanding safety and survival methods may make a significant difference in an emergency. Consider reading:

- **"Mountaineering:** The Freedom of the Hills" is a famous textbook on hiking and climbing skills.

- **"Wilderness Survival"** by Dave Canterbury teaches practical survival techniques for the wilderness.

3. Online Resources

Websites and blogs provide current information and personal experiences. Recommended websites include:

- **Backpacker.com** provides route evaluations, gear suggestions, and hiking information.

- REI Co-op Journal offers articles about hiking, gear, and outdoor skills.

4. Trail-specific Resources

For further information on individual trails or localities, see trail organization websites or local outdoor organizations. These frequently include current trail conditions, maps, and event information.

Hiking Termologies

Understanding hiking lingo might help you improve your route experience and communicate with other hikers. Here is a dictionary of essential words.

1. Trail Terminology

• A blaze is a mark on a tree or rock that shows the path route.

• Switchbacks are trails that zigzag up a steep slope.

• The trailhead is the starting point of a path.

• **Elevation Gain:** The overall amount of climbing done during a hike.

2. Gear Terminology

• The base layer of clothes is worn against the skin to wick away sweat.

• **Insulation Layer:** Clothing that retains body heat, such fleece or down coats.

• **Hydration System:** Gear such as hydration packs or bottles for carrying and drinking water while trekking.

3. Safety terminology

• **Shelter:** A tent or emergency bivvy provides protection from the elements.

• Hypothermia is a hazardous decline in body temperature caused by prolonged exposure to cold.

• **Dehydration:** Lack of fluid intake might create health complications.

Useful Apps & Tools for Hikers

Modern technologies may greatly improve your hiking experience. Here's a list of programs and tools that I find very helpful:

1. Navigation Apps

• AllTrails provides accurate trail maps, user reviews, and GPS tracking. Ideal for exploring new paths and organizing treks.

• Gaia GPS offers topographic maps, offline navigation, and tracking tools. Perfect for backwoods trekking.

2. Weather Apps

• Weather Underground offers reliable weather predictions and notifications for your trekking area.

• **Mountain Weather**: Provides customized weather updates for mountainous areas.

3. First Aid Apps

• The American Red Cross's First Aid guide offers step-by-step guidance for handling common injuries and situations.

• Wilderness First Aid provides extensive knowledge for treating injuries and diseases in isolated regions.

4. Fitness Tracking Apps

• Strava tracks hiking routes, speed, and distances. Ideal for tracking your progress and creating objectives.

• Use Map My Hike for full hiking data and route planning.

Having access to credible materials, learning hiking lingo, and utilizing current applications and technologies may help make your hiking trips safer and more pleasant. This appendix is intended to offer you with the necessary knowledge to traverse the trails, keep informed, and make the most of your outdoor adventures.

Whether you're a seasoned hiker or just getting started, keeping these tools on hand and familiarizing yourself with them can help you overcome any problem that arises. Stay prepared, educated, and most importantly, enjoy every step of your hiking adventure. Best wishes!

Map Of The Missouri Trails

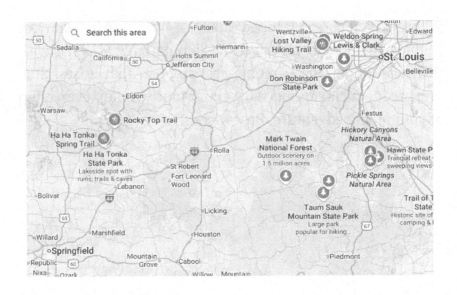

Scan The QR Code With Your Smart Phone
To Get The Locations In Real Time

https://maps.app.goo.gl/C9jk15596Nah1i
db7

Things To Do In The Missouri Trails

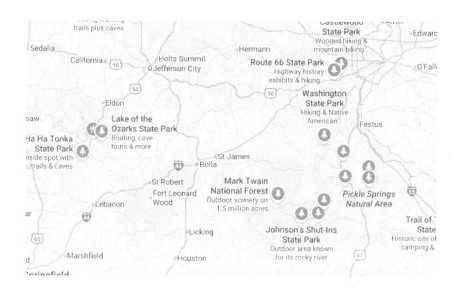

Scan The QR Code With Your Smart Phone
To Get The Locations In Real Time

https://maps.app.goo.gl/oTe4HsXiSW2D
NRkK8

Restaurants In The Missouri Trails

Scan The QR Code With Your Smart Phone
To Get The Locations In Real Time

https://maps.app.goo.gl/PGReNAcrhraToGjPA

Pharmacies In The Missouri Trails

Scan The QR Code With Your Smart Phone
To Get The Locations In Real Time

https://maps.app.goo.gl/dqpkutHhAm6LYfxY7

Made in the USA
Coppell, TX
11 December 2024

42229872R00138